THE HEARHIP FILES

The Heart of Worship Files

compiled by
MATT REDMAN

survivor

First published 2003
Reprint 2004

ISBN 1 84291 136 8

03 04 05 06 07 PRINTING / YEAR 09 08 07 06

Published by
KINGSWAY COMMUNICATIONS LTD
Lottbridge Drove, Eastbourne BN23 6NT, England.
Email: books@kingsway.co.uk

Printed in United States.

Contents

Intro

The church today is full of new songs and sounds. Look around and you'll find so many creative approaches to leading worship – signs of love and life from an adoring bride. We are a singing church. We journey on for the kingdom come, treading with reverence and shouting for joy. It's an exciting time to be involved in leading God's people in worship through music. Into this environment heartofworship.com was born – an online resource to encourage, challenge and inspire lead worshippers along the way. *The Heart of Worship Files* is a collection of highlights from the website.

There are many different sides to leading worship, so this book has been compiled with that in mind, giving practical advice for the pastoral aspects of worship leading, creative advice for the musical side of things, and perceptive insights into the theology of worship, as well as delving into our heritage for some inspiration from musical worshippers of the past. Throughout the book you'll also find a recurring section called 'The one thing . . .'. Here experienced lead worshippers have given their response to the question: 'What is the one thing most on your heart for those involved in leading worship these days?'

Some of the material in this book is a fairly light-hearted read and pretty easy to get to grips with. Other sections might require a little more serious study. We hope this mixture will both inspire and instruct you in your walk of worship.

Most of all, we pray that these highlights from heartofworship.com will sharpen you in your quest to know Jesus and make Him known to others.

Matt Redman

key words of mutual importance

Revelation and Response

Matt Redman

Recently I've been considering worship through the windows of 'revelation' and 'response'. What kind of revelation do the songs we use bring to the people who sing them? Do they paint a 'big' picture of God? Is there enough of His grace and splendour in our worship meetings to awaken even tired, discouraged hearts? And are we responding in a way that fits the revelation received? Worship is always a response to a revelation.

As I look at these two aspects of worship, I see I've paid more attention to one than the other. I often find myself approaching congregational worship much more mindful of the response element than of the revelation side of things. And I wonder if that isn't the case for many other lead worshippers too.

In some church services it's obvious the worship leader is above all else consumed with getting a response from the people. Not much is implied about the integrity and heart of the offerings. Instead comes a barrage of forceful encouragements to 'shout/clap/dance' and anything else they can think of. Instead of focusing on bringing a true and meaningful overflow of the heart, it seems instead they've settled for some sort of spiritual disco competition, with a prize for the wildest participant. Yet it's easy to point the finger. Am I so very different when I lead worship? What's going on inside my head when I lead?

Haven't I led in meetings where at the end of every celebration song my mind gets the 'clap-o-meter' out to check if we're on course? After all, if people clap at the end of each up-tempo song, that means we're in for a good meeting, doesn't it? Don't I sometimes find myself subconsciously scanning the congregational horizon for any sign of life? (Some outstretched hands would definitely mean it's working!) As we move into intimate reverence, don't I sometimes squint through my half-closed eyes to see what other responses are happening, hoping to see at least one person on their knees or in tears?

I'm exaggerating to make a point, but I hope the point is clear. Too often when I lead worship I'm driven by getting a good response out of the people. I want to see results.

Now, all of these things are potentially good things – dancing, lifting up holy hands, clapping, kneeling – but rather than being so desperate to see these things happen (or, God forbid, even trying to make them happen) I should be far more interested in what lies behind these responses (or the lack of them). It's a subtle distinction, but an important one for the mindset of any lead worshipper.

And that takes us right back to revelation. Before we

become consumed with how people are responding, it's good to be mindful of what they're responding to. As worship leaders and songwriters, we need to pay more attention to the reasons for God's worth in our writing and leading. What aspects of His wonders and splendour are we presenting for people to get their hearts into? How are we reminding hearts, minds and souls of the merciful acts that have been done for them, and the amazing grace that has been won for them?

Now, of course, this isn't just our responsibility, because everyone involved in the service plays a part. But we must take our role seriously. Instead of trying to work people up, however subtly, to some sort of response, let's take a different approach. Let's bring songs so full of our glorious Jesus that they ignite a fresh fire and a heart-filled response from those who sing them.

William Temple once wrote:

> Worship is to quicken the conscience by the holiness of God,
> To feed the mind with the truth of God,
> To purge the imagination by the beauty of God,
> To devote the will to the purpose of God.

Notice how much his definition of worship is centred around revelation. Here's a man who knew that to get people caught up in the holiness, truth and beauty of God results in the devotion of the will to the purpose of God – our whole lives poured out in worship. And in the end, that is the ultimate response of anyone who has truly recognised the all-consuming revelation of God.

If, in the power of the Holy Spirit, we can help usher people into a fresh revelation of Jesus during our worship times, the response will take care of itself. We will not be able to stand in the way of a room of passionate, dancing, shouting, bowing, adoring lovers of God.

the one thing...

Graham Kendrick

Pursue the biggest vision of Christ you can. My reference Bible records 101 different names and titles by which He is revealed in the Bible, each one a key to knowing more of who it is we are worshipping and why. Worship is a response and will grow or shrink in direct proportion to our view of Him. We love to worship Him as Saviour and Friend, but how often do we worship Him as Judge, or Author of Life, or Desired of All Nations? Seek out, use and, if you are able, write truth-saturated songs that stretch the minds and hearts of the worshipping church to grasp as much as we can of His incredible glories and cosmic purposes.

Little Leaders – A Reflection on Psalm 8: Part 1

Louie Giglio

O Lord, our Lord, how majestic is your name in all the earth. (Psalm 8:1)

When worship is the subject, little leaders are what we need. I don't mean small in stature, but small in terms of self. For there is no greater enemy of true worship than self.

As a result of the Fall we all have a deadly preoccupation with ourselves. We are self-aware, self-focused, self-conscious, self-made, self-protecting, self-promoting, self-centred and selfish. Conversion to Christ is nothing less than getting over ourselves. That's why there is more than a subtle change that must happen at the foot of the cross. A death takes place there. For Christianity is not about self-help but about self-death. New life begins when we abandon ourselves and fall on the mercy of a God who loved us in spite of ourselves and a Christ who gave Himself in our place. In that moment, we embrace freedom from the perpetual doom of the flesh and take up the cause of living solely for the One who frees us. Such is the way of the Saviour, calling any would-be recipient of new life to 'Deny yourself, take up your cross daily, and follow me'.

Yet from my experience self does not go quietly. Instead, it stubbornly rears its head and demands its way, looking for any opportunity to stand in the limelight and receive the glory. If left unchecked, self will stand in the light of God and somehow try to take credit for it.

Recently, I was stunned by a photograph in *USA Today* of what astronomers say is 'the perfect spiral galaxy'. Taken with the help of a new telescope on the Big Island of Hawaii, the photo shows a breathtaking shot of a galaxy named NGC 628, which is slightly smaller than our Milky Way (it contains only a paltry 100 billion stars) and, get this, 30 million light years away. The whole point of the article was man's great achievement in that *we* took such a great photograph with *our* two-week-old telescope. Aren't *we* great? Hmm. Seems like all the wrong pronouns to me! Granted, we have done well to photograph anything 30 million light years away, but let's be clear: God's hand put every one of those stars in place. A better caption would have been 'Can You Believe God Made This Stuff With His Own Hands?'

So the psalmist writes:

When I consider your heavens, the work of your fingers, the moon and the stars, which you have set in place, what is man that you are mindful of him, or the son of man that you care for him? (Psalm 8:3–4)

Notice all the pronouns: *Your* heavens, *Your* fingers, *You* have set in place. God is far from small. In fact, it is safe to say that our self-limitation has never fully allowed us to think of Him as He is. Given His incomprehensible immensity, the fact that He is mindful of us at all is amazing!

So if you want a quick glimpse into how small you come across as a leader, take note of which pronouns consume you: His, He and Yours, or I, me and mine. Little leaders use 'He' a lot. The big ones use 'me'.

A stage is a dangerous place to be, for by definition it is a raised platform. Stages are built so that little people can be seen more easily by larger audiences. The lights are bright. The sound is big. Yet if we are not careful, those of us who lead worship can allow the stage to succeed, making more of us than we really are. It's not that we are nobodies. We're created a little lower than angels and are crowned with glory and honour (made in His image). We get to rule over all He has made. But we've only to look up to be re-sized in an instant.

Rather than absorb the light that shines on leaders, we must continually reflect it back to God. One night my wife Shelley and I were flying home from Houston to Waco in a small twin-engine plane. Every time I looked out of the window I saw a massive searchlight moving rapidly across the ground below. At first I thought a police helicopter was tracking some criminals, but after an hour the light was still there. Finally, I spoke up, wondering aloud what could be going on. The pilot, ever so confident, informed me that the moon (which was full at the time and pretty much right there if only I'd looked up) was shining on the plane, reflecting a huge circle of light to the ground.

I felt like an idiot! Embarrassed and a little humiliated, I went back to minding my own business. Then it hit me! Eager to get even, I remarked that actually the moon was not shining on the plane, but rather the sun was shining on the moon and the light of the sun was reflecting off the moon onto the plane. Thus the sunlight was making the huge 'searchlight' on the ground. Brilliant!

So as far as lead worshippers go, we need more little moons. Shine a light on them if you will, but you'll only see a greater reflection of His glory in all those around them.

O Lord, our Lord, how majestic is your name in all the earth! (Psalm 8:1)

the one thing...

Mike Pilavachi

The question that has challenged me recently is: 'How many songs do we sing that are just about God and do not bring us into the story? How much is God not only the object but also the centre of our worship?' I am sure we need to sing more songs that praise Him for who He is, irrespective of what He has done for us. The worship of heaven, as we see in Revelation 4 and 5, is amazing in its colour, sound and participants. The four living creatures and the twenty-four elders seem to be having a great time as they take it in turns to sing their songs and fall down. A few million angels and then every creature join them. Great sight. Great noise. But incomplete. The centrepiece comes as the grand finale: the One who sits on the throne, and the Lamb. The rest is incidental, the audience, the supporting cast.

How God-centred is my worship? Maybe I need to tell Him a little less about me – what I feel and what I am going to do – and focus a little more on Him.

creative insight

Worship and Addiction

Don Williams

Worship money and you will become a greedy person. Worship sex and you will become a lustful person. Worship power and you will become a corrupt person. Worship Jesus and you will become a Christ-like person. We become like the object of our worship. But what does it mean to worship?

The verb 'worship' in Hebrew means to surrender, to fall down in submission – the way we would humble ourselves before a mighty king (Psalm 95:6).[1] Paul says that worship is the offering of our bodies as a sacrifice (Romans 12:1). This worship goes on in all of our lives. While we may fail to understand it, worship is the spiritual part of our surrender, submission and attachment to many things. The worship of money or sex or power or people results in addictive and compulsive behaviours. The staggering truth is that we are all lured into worshipping something or someone other than the living God. This is idolatry, pure and simple. It steals our humanity and addicts us. So if we are truly to be free from idolatry, we must understand addiction.

Addiction happens when we attach our desire to someone or something that controls us. As that attachment grows, it consumes us. Little by little, we become captive to the very things that give us pleasure and meaning. Dr Gerald May says, 'We are all addicts in every sense of the word.'[2] If this is true, we are also all idolaters in every sense of the word. You might deny this, but remember that denial is the first symptom of addiction.

Psychologist John Bradshaw says that most of us come from 'dysfunctional' families, families that don't work in an open, healthy way. We were often abused as children, either sexually, physically or verbally. We live with a lot of repressed pain as a result. Bradshaw calls this 'the hole in the soul'.[3] We will stuff anything into it in order to fill it up. It is a magnet for addictions. But it only grows larger, because nothing satisfies.

If idolatry is the issue and addiction the result, how can we understand it? The three Cs provide a handle. Addiction starts with *craving*. It leads to *control loss* and the result is *continuing use*. We build, say, a dependency on nicotine. When we need a fix, to relax us or lift our mood, the craving sets in. The more we use, the more we want (and need). We are now out of control, on our way to chain smoking. Once addicted we are in the continual use pattern. When this becomes an obsession, it becomes an idol.

What then is the root of addiction? It is spiritual; it is

idolatry. Whatever the objects of our addiction are, they become idols in our lives. We become preoccupied with them, crave them, serve them. As we have seen, worshipping them is the spiritual side of addiction. The Bible teaches that we not only dishonour God with our idols, but we also lose our true humanity: '. . . their idols are silver and gold, made by the hands of men. . . . Those who make them will be like them, and so will all who trust in them' (Psalm 115:4–8); 'They followed worthless idols and became worthless themselves' (Jeremiah 2:5b).

In *New Tasks for a Renewed Church*, Tom Wright analyses idolatry.[4] First, idols are all a perversion of the good. For example, sex is good, under God's design and plan, but as an idol, it is degraded and enslaves us. Second, idols enhance us. When we worship them, we feel ten feet tall. Third, idols demand sacrifice. Every addict knows what she or he has sacrificed to the idol of alcohol or drugs – time, energy, money, integrity and even other people. Fourth, we create an ideology to justify our idols. Sexual obsession becomes the sexual revolution, the conquest of damaging, Victorian repression. Fifth, idols enslave us. They demand our lives. No wonder Paul teaches that behind the dumb idols lurk demons (1 Corinthians 10:19–20). They want to hold us in the kingdom of darkness.

The Bible carries on a continual battle with idolatry. The first commandment is: 'You shall have no other gods before me.' The second is: 'You shall not make for yourself an idol in the form of anything . . .' (Exodus 20:3–4).

God alone is worthy of our worship. In this, He gives us back our true selves.

If we become what we worship, the road out of idolatry is to renounce our idols and turn to the living God. This begins with a personal, public surrender. In psychological language, we must 'detach'. This can only come by God's gracious intervention. Moral conviction will not do it. Only brokenness at the centre of our being will do it. Only cutting through our shame and guilt will do it.

Paul writes in Romans 12:1: 'Therefore, I urge you, brothers, in view of God's mercy, to offer your bodies as living sacrifices, holy and pleasing to God – this is your spiritual act of worship.' By this mercy, then, we come to worship. We bring the sacrifice of our bodies. They are acceptable to God, through the perfect, sinless body of His Son.

Now we ask the Spirit of God to fill the 'hole in the soul' with Himself. We begin to worship God alone – to love Him with all our heart, mind, soul and strength. This worship will change us into Christ-likeness. Rather than being conformed to this world and our idolatrous addictions, He will conform us to Himself (Romans 12:2). Worship drugs and you become a depressed or burned-out person. Worship work and you become a restless, frantic person. Worship people and you become a selfish, dependent person. Worship Jesus and you become a Christ-like person.

We are either like the idols or like the living God. We must make our choice. Paul tells the Thessalonians: '. . . you turned to God from idols to serve the living and true God, and to wait for his Son from heaven, whom he raised from the dead – Jesus, who rescues us from the coming wrath' (1 Thessalonians 1:9–10). There really is no option.

the one thing...

Sally Morgenthaler

As a young worship leader, I focused on creating worship experiences; on making sure people felt as though they'd met God before they left. As a worship planner, I still ask myself the question 'How are people going to encounter God in this time of worship?' But increasingly I'm focusing on the God of our experience, not the experience itself, because it's entirely possible to feel close to God without really focusing on who God is. It's entirely possible to work ourselves into a worship euphoria without distinguishing between God-Generic and God-Incarnate. And in this age of spiritual pluralism, that difference is pivotal. Do we lead people into the throne room of a generic God, or do we draw them into the presence of the One revealed and made eternally accessible to us in Jesus Christ?

Let us introduce a waiting world to the Father. But may it be only through the Son and by the power of the Holy Spirit. Worship leading is more than crafting awesome God experiences. It is introducing people to the awesome God of the experience: Creator, Redeemer and Sustainer.

Making Melody: Songwriting Part 1

There are perhaps two main types of melody-writer: those who stumble across tunes (like me), and those who know about music theory, and might therefore take a more thought-out approach. Whichever type you are, make sure you write from your heart.

The best congregational melodies work *in* worship because they began *as* worship. Write songs that are easy to learn and hard to forget – melodies that can be memorised straight away, yet also have a catchy, lingering tune that stays in your head long after the moment.

One other thing: in most types of music, the chords are just as important as the melody line itself. It's always good to run the melody line through several different chord progressions, just to see what happens. You may sometimes come across a beautiful match between tune and chord that you weren't planning originally.

Matt Redman

Be yourself. Let the melody flow naturally from your personality. Don't evaluate too quickly. You can't be self-conscious at this stage – you must let yourself 'feel'. Mechanical melodies don't move people – human ones do. I find I need some space, time and privacy at this point – I can't be thinking about someone listening. I just have to 'let go', which usually means singing some things that sound odd. Once the basic melody is there, step back and evaluate: Is it memorable? Is there a strong motif holding each section of the song together?

Finally, make sure your high point melodically is your high point lyrically. It doesn't really help the song if your highest and climactic note comes on the word 'and'!

Brian Doerksen

Of course, everyone has a different approach to this. I once heard Willie Nelson (an American folk legend!) say that melodies are all around us in the air; we just have to grab them. I like that. It's a bit abstract, but it's a good picture. When grabbing for one of them, keep your congregation in mind. Remember that most people are musically illiterate. Keep the rhythm of the lyrics simple. Try to create space within the song. While you should keep in mind the vocal ranges for both men and women, it's sometimes appropriate to place melodies on the edge of these ranges to cause people to really sing out.

Chris Tomlin

Listen to many styles of music. Having a wide range of musical input increases your chances of good musical output. Secondly, try to develop melody without your instrument. This can help you to avoid getting stuck in a 'playing rut', where one chord always naturally progresses to another. Thirdly, try sometimes to write melody and lyrics together as this can help form the direction and tone of the song.

Martyn Layzell

Match the language of the words with that of the music, so that the melody brings to life the text, and the text enhances the music.

There are limitless possibilities in the composition of melody. A great deal can be communicated with very little. The intervals of the notes within a melody, whether based on the modal system, the major and minor scales, or perhaps influenced by Indian or Oriental scales, create a language and mood of impression.

As composers and writers of melody in the sphere of sacred music, we must make time to quietly listen to the language that speaks to our hearts and minds – the still small voice of our great and wonderful God of love, our inspirational Creator. In humility of heart and purpose we may then bring something of heaven down to earth in our music. Our duty and our joy is to put new melodies and inspiring heavenly music onto the lips and into the hearts of God's children.

Dave Clifton

Work with 'hooks'. In other words, a little melody that hooks itself in your head. We all know songs that have good hooks; they're the ones we remember and want to sing over and over. You only need one or two hooks in a song, and as long as the rest of the melody is good, it will 'sing' really well. Also, make sure the melody is simple enough to learn yet interesting enough for people to want to sing time and again.

Kathryn Scott

It is very hard to put into words the process of writing a melody. Personally I need to record all of my ideas and then give them time to form. I have a mini-disc packed full of song ideas. It takes me weeks, even months, to form these tunes fully. The temptation is to rush it and assume a tune is finished. Melodies can almost always be improved.

The key thing in evaluating a melody is to ask yourself, 'Is it singable?' Is it a tune you enjoy singing, and find catchy even when you sing it away from your instrument? If so, you're on to something! This issue of 'singability' is crucial. You can have the most inspired, poetic lyrics, drenched in biblical truth, but if the tune is dull or awkward to sing, it may never work as a congregational worship song.

Tim Hughes

Delightful or Dreadful?

Steve Nicholson

As a pastor I have been working with worship leaders for over twenty-five years. Generally it has been a positive experience. My current worship pastor and I have been working together for twelve years and look forward to many more. Yet there have been times when my interactions with worship leaders have left me groaning inside. So what's the difference? What makes some such a delight and others such a sorrow?

You might expect me to focus on the intricacies of pastor/worship leader relationships, but this time I'd like to assume that there are no problems there and focus on other qualities: three to delight in, three to dread.

Qualities to delight in

1. A love for worshipping Jesus that is readily seen

There is nothing quite so powerful as worshipping under the leadership of someone who really loves worshipping

Jesus and somehow has the ability to let that be seen by the congregation. It doesn't have to be over the top, it just has to be genuine and expressed somehow. Sometimes it's just a matter of how the songs are sung. Sometimes it's a matter of how songs are chosen. Not everyone who genuinely loves worship is able to let others see it from the stage and then participate in it. But when that does happen, even the simplest songs can take us to heaven.

2. A commitment to being a functioning disciple and church member who happens to lead worship sometimes

Worship leaders need to be genuinely connected to their churches and this needs to be evidenced by things like staying and listening to the sermons rather than hiding backstage when not leading worship; joining in the prayer times; building relationships with those who are not musicians; being open about their need to keep growing in Christ and learning, even though they spend a lot of time on stage. This will not only serve as a great protection for the worship leader's spiritual and moral life, it will also prevent elitism.

3. A healthy balance between hanging on to the tried and true ways and songs of worship from the past, and a continual development of fresh ways of worshipping God

If their worship is not to become routine and stagnant, congregations need a continual (but not too steep) growth curve – fresh ways of worshipping God, including new songs. At the same time we need to stay connected to the best of the past, both the more recent past and the past of previous generations. This is going to require a lot of study, research and work on the part of the worship leader, but over the long haul it will help produce a healthier congregation of worshippers.

Qualities to dread

1. The performance mentality

It is all too easy for worship leaders to become rock 'n' roll stars who perform songs with Christian lyrics. The focus then shifts onto the music, and we end up with a show that lacks any thought for whether this is helping the folk in the back row get connected with God in worship. When this performance mentality starts to take hold, it is usually seen in a kind of elitism – acting like a professional band: hiding out backstage or elsewhere when not leading worship (i.e. the music is the only time/way that the worship leader is involved with the church/congregation); hanging out only with musicians; doing things because they 'showcase' talents rather than because they help ordinary people worship; or, even more subtle, doing songs that are difficult to sing by untrained musicians. All these things will ultimately infect the church with attitudes likely to kill genuine worship of Jesus.

2. The 'lone ranger' mentality

I have seen some worship leaders – leaders who genuinely love worshipping Jesus – leave the congregation way behind as they go off into the heights of their own personal worship and creativity. They are having a good worship experience, it seems, but only a few others can manage to join with them. This can happen when songs are too complex to sing, or when the worship leader goes off into long impromptu worship, leaving the congregation wondering what they are supposed to sing/do next. I have seen some worship leaders drift off into 'the wide blue yonder' with their eyes shut for thirty to forty minutes, not once noticing that 85 per cent of the congregation have lost the plot and are standing there watching them in silence.

It is important to remember that the job of the worship leader is to help a congregation of ordinary people, most of them not trained musicians, worship God in a meaningful and participatory way.

3. The 'artsy' mentality

By this I mean the attitude that conveys that it is more important for the worship leader to explore, develop and display his or her artistic and creative abilities than to help the people to enter into worship. Sometimes this is done in the name of attracting the artsy people who might come. But if the people who are already there and ready to worship God are excluded in the process, nothing of lasting value is going to be accomplished. There are perhaps good places for this exploration of artistic ability to take place, but a worship service is not one of them – unless one has a unique congregation of nothing but musicians and artistic people.

All these qualities, both positive and negative, are based on actual experiences I have had. The fact that you're reading this means you're already genuinely concerned with how to grow and to be a good worship leader. But my hope is that this will encourage you to keep developing in the three delightful qualities here, while watching out for the three dreadful ones.

the one thing...

John Willison

Short of loving Jesus Himself, the one thing I'd say is to love the church, His bride. Carry the church in your heart – all the different people, and all the different kinds of people. Think about her during your day. Love her. Protect her. Honour her. Don't let anyone use her, abuse her, say anything bad about her. Make your decisions for the betterment of the church – your songs, your list, your personnel and your training of others.

Only let people who truly love the church serve the church and lead the church.

Refreshing Hymns

Matt Redman

Have you ever been leading worship and not able to find the right song for that moment? Maybe a song of lament was needed, but you didn't really know any. Or the pastor asked for a song responding to the holiness of God, but again you couldn't seem to find an appropriate one for that theme.

If you're anything like me, you'll have been in this kind of situation a few times. I'm realising more and more that as worship leaders we need to widen our 'song vocabulary' to include songs for every biblical theme and songs for every walk of life.

In the light of this, I've been delving into a few old hymn books, and I've been seeing a depth and breadth of lyrical content that we cannot afford to ignore. As worship leaders we have an amazing heritage. Throughout the ages many of the saints have poured their hearts out to God through song. So many of these hymns and songs resound with our hearts even now. It's faith-building too to realise that hundreds of years ago these writers were meeting with, and responding to, the very same Jesus we encounter today. So many of these old hymn-writers and their hymns have much to teach us about writing poetic, biblical songs, and I for one have decided I want to become their student. I'm hungry for everything I can get my hands on.

A friend of mine recently gave me a copy of an old Methodist hymn book he found in the attic. The book is a collection of 'Methodist Protestant' hymns, published in Baltimore, USA, in 1849. As soon as I opened the first page I knew I was in for an education. I have never seen such a diverse collection of biblical themes in one book.

The first section goes through the 'Attributes of God', and includes His wisdom, holiness, justice, goodness, truth, faithfulness, trinity, mercy, love, eternity, omnipresence and omnipotence. Pretty impressive. But that's only the start. Next up we discover a list of hymns on the 'Relations of God' (in other words who He is to us), and here we find the subjects 'Maker', 'Preserver' and 'Sovereign'.

We then get onto the 'Works of God'. This comes in three sections: Creation, Providence and Redemption. In this third section there are hymns covering every imaginable angle of our redemption: love of the Father, character of Christ, promise of Christ, types of Christ, birth of Christ, life of Christ, death of Christ, resurrection of Christ, ascension of Christ, intercession of Christ, reign of Christ, second coming of Christ, offices of Christ and titles of Christ. Again, a pretty extensive list!

The next section has twelve pages of hymns that respond to, and call on, the Holy Spirit: songs on the promise of the Holy Spirit, the descent of the Holy Spirit, the operations of the Spirit, prayer for the Spirit and addresses to the Spirit.

Let me warn you: at this point we are not even a third of the way through the hymn book! Next we get into songs about the church – songs for times of revival in church, and songs for times of 'declension' (when things aren't going too great).

Then the themes just keep on coming: songs of salvation, songs of repentance, songs of faith, justification and our adoption. Songs of hope, humility, joy, love, wisdom, the mind of Christ, triumph in death, glory in the resurrection, immortality in heaven, and worshipping God for His judgements.

Then we get down to the 'Private Devotion' section: hymns to sing before you go to bed, and songs to sing when you read the Bible. Songs to sing at morning, noon, evening and midnight!

Finally, we get to the last few sections, which provide songs of response to God for other situations we may find ourselves in. Songs that describe the Christian life as 'a pilgrimage', 'a race' and 'warfare'. Songs for times of affliction: poverty, persecution, temptation, sickness and bereavement. Then some songs for particular occasions: fast days, funerals, prayer nights, New Year, meetings for the poor and missionary meetings. There's even a little section of songs for 'the backslider'!

When I look at a 150-year-old collection of worship

songs like this, it inspires and encourages me to want to press on and take my songwriting a little more seriously. The church needs songs that help us respond to God in worship as we walk out our lives before Him. Songs that get to grips with all the wonderful facets of His nature, character and splendour. Songs that provide an entry point for the person who doesn't know Him. Songs that respond to, revere and call upon the Holy Spirit, who with the Father and Son is worshipped and glorified. There are so many more ways I could respond to my God in song.

Let us build up a greater vocabulary of songs, that we might more worthily magnify His name and more capably serve God's church as lead worshippers.

the one thing...

Darlene Zschech

The one thing I'm increasingly aware of is the spiritual responsibility given to us by our Lord and King. He has trusted us with this season in history. We need to grow up as leaders in the things of God – not easily shaken, and immovable in our pursuit of bringing heaven to earth. Lead worshippers who bring faith and annihilate fear; who bring dancing and tread on mourning; who bring courage and break down discouragement – in spirit and truth – for the glory of God.

Understanding Worship: Part 1
Chris Jack

Christians all do it. Sometimes we enjoy it. Often we don't, if we're really honest about it. Why do we bother? What's the point? Is there something better we could be doing with our time?

We're talking about worship, of course, and it's a subject that frequently gives rise to heated debate. For we all have our preferences; we all know just how it should be done, and how it shouldn't! In this, as in many other areas of life, we know what we like, what appeals to us, what suits our tastes. And there is plenty of choice on offer: traditional, contemporary, liturgical, charismatic, alternative, blended – seemingly something for everyone. As the song goes, 'I did it my way'.

But what happens when *my* way isn't *your* way and we're both in the same congregation? Tensions develop. Factions emerge. And before you know it you are in a war zone. The phrase now coined to describe this kind of situation is 'Worship wars'. Sadly, such wars are common in our day, causing much disruption and at times real hurt in our churches. Battles rage in particular around musical preferences.

But is this really what it's all about? In our focus on how we worship maybe we've missed the point. Don't we first need to think about what worship is, and why we worship? Surely it is only as we understand the 'what' and the 'why' of worship that we can properly begin to address the 'how'. Yet we persist with our disputes over styles of worship as though this is what matters most. In truth, much of the time we merely defend our personal preferences, however much we might endeavour to clothe our arguments in suitable theological garb.

> Confusion abounds in our postmodern world concerning the nature of Christian worship. (Constance Cherry)

Biblically, worship is all about responding in right ways to God. And the first thing we must grasp is that worship is primarily about God. While we may readily pay lip service to this fact, in practice it is often quite difficult for us to engage with. We live in a very self-centred world, where self-gratification, self-satisfaction, self-fulfilment and the like drive so much of our activity, and determine so many of our responses. If we're not careful, we'll find ourselves evaluating our worship in this self-focused way. Of course worship involves me – I am a participant in it – yet it is not primarily about me or for me.

There are three key biblical reasons for worship. Note that, significantly, all are God-focused.

1. God deserves our worship

Worship is a right and fitting response to God, both because of who He is and because of what He has done. This is a constant motif throughout Scripture, finding particular expression in the Psalms (see, e.g., Psalms 98, 100, 104, 111). We worship God in His infinite greatness and goodness, recognising His superiority to us in every way; and we worship Him for His great acts as Creator and Redeemer. Something of this is vividly portrayed in Revelation 4–5, a passage which affords a glorious glimpse of the true worship taking place in heaven.

2. God requires our worship

The relationship between God and His people, under both the old and the new covenant, is established by God's initiative and on God's terms. In the Old Testament, the Law given at Sinai is in effect a statement of the terms of the covenant. Within this statement is enshrined the command to worship God. It is implicit in the Ten Commandments (Exodus 20:1ff.) and made explicit elsewhere (e.g. Exodus 23:25; Deuteronomy 6:13 [cf. Matthew 4:10]). And in the New Testament there is no less focus on worship as a covenant requirement (e.g. John 4:22–24; Romans 12:1; Hebrews 12:28). Furthermore, God's new covenant people are described as 'a royal priesthood', whose very calling is to 'declare the praises' of God (1 Peter 2:9). So worship is a requirement, a duty (and therefore something to be done irrespective of how we *feel*, as a response of our will), as well as a natural and fitting response to God that flows spontaneously from our minds and our hearts. Either way, it is about Him and for Him!

3. God enables our worship

Finally, it's worth noting that worship is only possible because God has made it so. It is He who decisively revealed Himself throughout the Old Testament and who has finalised that revelation in the person of His Son, Jesus Christ (John 1:18). And it is He who, in Christ, has opened up a new basis for relationship with Himself (2 Corinthians 5:17–21), offering direct access into His presence (Ephesians 2:18; Hebrews 10:19–22). The remarkable thing is that on the basis of Christ's once-for-all sacrifice of Himself, God accepts our worship and even delights in it (Romans 12:1; Philippians 4:18). What is important to underline here is that worship, in all its forms and expressions, is first and foremost for God's pleasure, not ours.

The remarkable irony is that when we get this perspective right – when we worship God for the right reasons, on His terms and as He has enabled us to – the result is that we can truly enjoy Him as He intends we should. Notwithstanding the exclusive language, the extract from the Westminster Shorter Catechism (seventeenth century) below still holds as a poignantly succinct statement of why we should worship God: it is what we were made for.

What is the chief end of man? Man's chief end is to glorify God, and to enjoy Him for ever. (Westminster Shorter Catechism)

the one thing...

Brian Doerksen

Worship is an act of love. The great thing is that no two people express love in exactly the same way. How has God made you to express love? That is where the power will be!

Where Are All God's Celebrity Chefs?

David Salmon

When it comes to learning about worship, most of us head straight to the Psalms for some inspiration. But let me ask you this: does your church overhead ever project the words from some of the more 'difficult' psalms? There are plenty of straight-down-the-line 'Praise the Lord' style psalms of course, but what do you do when you stumble across a rant from some disgruntled priest in Psalm 73? Why the story about ships being wrecked at sea in Psalm 107, and why the catalogue of failures from Israel's past in Psalm 106?

The Psalms weren't just the ballads of self-indulgent songwriters, never to be heard in public. They were as much part of temple worship as the more famous songs of praise, like Psalm 150. And the truth is, they knew something that we in the twenty-first century often overlook: truth that seeps out from the cracks of 'stories' is absorbed deeper into the human heart than truth told as 'objective fact'. What we glean from 'between the lines' of all we see around us can have a deeply profound effect upon us.

A quick scan through the Bible shows that God seems to have chosen this way to communicate His truth to us. Between the two covers we find stories, histories, allegories, poetry, a play, ballads, transcripts of historical letters and wildly symbolic visionary prose. God, throughout the Old Testament, spoke to the prophets in pictures, painting rich images of deep revelation. Jesus, when surrounded by an attentive audience, spoke to them in parables. He never spelled out the truth; rather He contextualised it into stories that all could understand. Even today, through the Holy Spirit, we're given pictures and symbols that communicate truth to us. It seems to run in the family – a kind of 'Father, Son and Holy Spirit' thing, a Trinity of storytelling. To learn through interpreting the world around us is built into the very way God has made us. We even dream in symbols.

We take in truths the same way we take in nutrients – they are extracted and absorbed naturally from the food we eat. Yet as a church we are so concerned about exactly what nutrients we need, we often forget what the meal should actually taste like. Our theological scientists in their research seminaries have spent years analysing the things we eat, distilling them down to their constituent parts, and then labelling them in systematic test tubes. It's vital that they do, because without their tireless work we wouldn't have such a clear idea of what is needed for a good healthy diet. But on the other hand, if it were left to them to come up with the menu, we would end up with a plateful of pills instead of, say, braised salmon fillet wrapped in prosciutto, with herbs, on a bed of spinach and yoghurt.

The repercussions of this way of taking in nutrients actually go further than simply creating more appetising meals. An iron supplement may be of some good, but iron, taken in by eating foods like spinach or tuna, is actually absorbed into the body more efficiently. Nutritionists will tell you that a fresh orange, as well as looking and tasting fantastic, is a lot better for you than a Vitamin C tablet.

The restaurant needs the creativity of its chefs; the church needs the creativity of its communicators to work skilfully with the ingredients it has, crafting images, inventing stories, telling parables, writing songs and painting pictures. Layered creations out of which seep the liberating truths of love and grace; the difficult truths of judgement and holiness; the deep paradoxes that make up our lives with God.

The wonderful thing about truth in this context is that it always speaks in a language your soul can understand. It will never violate your free will, and though it may challenge and confront, ultimately the choice is left to you. As Jesus said, 'Those who have ears, let them hear.' When asked by His disciples why He told stories, Jesus replied, 'Whenever someone has a ready heart for this, the insights and understandings flow freely. But if there is no readiness, any trace of receptivity soon disappears. That's why I tell stories: to create readiness, to nudge the people towards receptive insight' (Matthew 13, *The Message*).

If Jesus spoke to the crowds this way, should we not work hard at following His example? We live among a generation of people who want nothing to do with the church. Listen to many of them for long enough and you will discover that it's not so much the message they dislike, as the way they are told it. The world has had enough of being force-fed pills, and yet it remains in desperate need of the divine nutrients of which it has been starved for so long.

Is it because we fear we might miss some vital nutrients that we have lost sight of the meal through which these truths are most effectively absorbed into the body? Do we not trust the chefs? The answer is to embrace the theologians and give freedom to the artists. As co-workers with Christ, we must learn to dwell together in the same camp, and realise just how much we need each other.

The Bridegroom is calling all of mankind to His banqueting table, but where are His celebrity chefs?

the one thing...

Matt Redman

Sometimes it can be tempting to strive to do something significant. We find ourselves wanting to write a significant song that will touch many hearts, or lead a significant time of worship in which lives are truly changed. But we are not called to significance. Instead, the calling is to obedience. Look through the Bible and see how obedience reaps some major significant outcomes. Look at Moses or Noah, for example. Ultimately, look at Jesus, and the cross. The most significant act in all history was one of sheer humble, enduring obedience.

Whether we're called up the front or more behind the scenes, obedience is always significant in the eyes of God.

A Life of Consideration – A Reflection on Psalm 8: Part 2

Louie Giglio

'When I consider . . .' (v. 3). 'What is man?' (v. 4). Somewhere between these two phrases worship begins.

The life of worship is a life of consideration. In other words, creating time and space to think is essential for developing a lifestyle of God-sized worship. A life of consideration requires time to wonder. Time to dwell. Time to ponder. Time to look up.

The psalmist had plenty of time to consider. I guess you could say it was one of the fringe benefits of being a herder of sheep. His office was shrouded in huge sky; his nightly entertainment, the dancing heavens above. Alone and awake, he had lots of time to look up and wonder. Gazing at the endless universe above made his head spin. Looking up, he said, 'When I consider your heavens, the work of your fingers, the moon and the stars, which you have set in place, what is man that you are mindful of him . . .?' (Psalm 8:3–4).

Looking up is what worship is all about, especially for those of us who spend most of our time looking around. Have you ever noticed that when we look around at our circumstances they tend to deflate worship, not inspire it? Looking around we see frustration. We see unfinished tasks. We see imperfection and injustice. Disease. We also see a multitude of lesser gods.

But when we look up everything changes. Intrigued by the night sky David saw order. Looking up he was confronted with the Incomprehensible. The Eternal. The Mysterious. The Expansive. The Beautiful. He saw for ever black and brilliant light. On the darkest of nights the stars seemed to stoop to touch him. The blacker the night, the brighter they glowed. The more isolated his location, the closer they appeared.

And how they sang!

> Someone made us, fancy that!
> And He knows us each by name.
> Here we hover, countless counted,
> spoken here to tell His fame.
>
> Stretch your mind, reach around us,
> though it's difficult we know.
> Stand in awe, drink in the wonder,
> join and sing our Maker's praise.

'O Lord, our Lord, how majestic is your name in all the earth!' (v. 1). For each of us worship begins as we intentionally create enough space to look up. No, it's not imperative that we spend a night alone with sheep. But it is essential that we take a deep breath, allowing our thoughts to drift from what is made to the One who makes it. We must take time to consider God.

Looking up, two things happen. God gets bigger and we get smaller. David wonders aloud, 'What is man that you are mindful of him . . . ?' That is the question we ask when we take time to consider. Instantly re-sized, we marvel at the wonder of it all. Seeing God arrayed in uncontainable splendour, we robe ourselves in humility, floored that we matter at all.

Non-considerers (I think I just invented that term) star in their own little universes, barely stopping to notice that their entire world, and all that captivates them, could easily fit on the head of the smallest of pins. But those who look up soon realise that they are in fact quite tiny, amazed that a God so big cares for those so small.

You see, David was looking up in amazement while at the same time having a conversation with the Architect of all he could see. I can hear him saying, 'What? Me – talking to You? How's that? I mean, who am I that I should even matter to You?'

But it's true. This ageless Creator has called us too by name, making us a little lower than the heavenly beings, crowning us with glory and honour, making us to rule over the work of His hands (see vv. 5–6).

Once again David feels so small. But it's a good small, not a bad small. In fact, it's a glorious small, which causes him to embrace his true value in the arms of a loving God, propelling him to offer unrestrained glory to the

Maker of all things. As Andrew Murray writes, 'It is only in the possession of God that I lose myself. As it is in the height and breadth and glory of the sunshine that the littleness of a spec of dust playing in the sunlight is seen, so humility is our being, in God's presence, nothing but a speck dwelling in the sunlight of His love.' He concludes: 'How great is God! How small am I! Lost, swallowed up in Love's immensity! God only there, not I' (Andrew Murray, *Humility*, Whitaker House, 1982).

There's a big, big God up there who knows your name. Just a little something for your consideration.

the one thing...

Brenton Brown

Never stop God from working on your heart just because you're up the front leading people in worship.

We often start out on this journey like a broken-down car, in need of repair. Most of us want to get the car totally sorted and fixed before we start the journey. But God says, 'Start the journey anyway. You'll find the service stations and mechanics on the way.' As we continue on the way into Him, periodically He pulls us aside and gives us a 'service', making us more and more like His Son. That's how this God-life works. But there's a real temptation when we become leaders to think that simply because we're at the front leading, our 'motors' are all sorted out and we don't need any more fixing. Of course that's not true. Leadership might mean we get to learn some of our lessons out front, in public, but it is never an excuse to stop learning and growing.

The Cross: Exploring all Angles

Don Williams

For the ancient world, crucifixion was the ultimate penalty. It included torture as well as capital punishment. To haul the cross to the place of execution, to hang naked, broken and bleeding was shameful enough. Then to die of suffocation, no longer able to support the body's weight on nailed hands or wrists, was horror in life, relieved only by death. No wonder the Romans called the cross 'the fatal wood', 'the infamous stake', 'the extreme penalty'. No citizen could normally be crucified. This death was the 'slave's punishment', reserved for aliens and outlaws. Legal terror contributed to Rome's obsession with controlling her far-flung empire. Now we understand why Paul says that the 'word of the cross' is folly to the Greeks and a scandal to the Jews (1 Corinthians 1:23). When he claims not to be ashamed of the gospel (Romans 1:16) he has every right to be. The word of the cross, Jesus Christ and Him crucified, is offensive for at least four reasons.

First, it is culturally offensive. No one speaks of the cross in polite society. That a god, eternal and immutable, could be crucified is crazy. Second, it is historically offensive. Christians claim that a peasant, itinerant Jew, legally and brutally executed under Roman law, is the Lord of the universe and the Saviour of the world. He alone deserves the exalted titles carried by the Emperor. Third, it is philosophically offensive. This is the 'offence of the particular'. Rather than the cross at best being an illustration of divine love, it is the basis for divine love. This particular cross establishes God's universal mercy and forgiveness for all. Fourth, it is morally offensive. To put it simply: you cannot save yourself. Salvation is only by faith in the crucified Jesus, atoning once for all for sin. The mangled Messiah is both God incarnate and the risen, reigning Lord.

With these offences, why did the earliest Christians glory in the cross? Shouldn't they have downplayed it for the sake of relevance, 'winning the right to be heard'? Why did they hold this bloody instrument up before the gaping ancient world?

The cross is the centre of the New Testament

The heart of the New Testament is not the ethic of Jesus, or the example of Jesus, or the wisdom of Jesus, or even the suffering service of Jesus. The heart of the New Testament is the cross, seen now through the lens of the risen, exalted Lord. Martin Kahler, in an overstatement, calls our four Gospels 'passion narratives with an introduction'.[1] Each one moves resolutely to Jesus' final week in Jerusalem: the plot against His life, His meal with His disciples establishing the new covenant in His body and blood, His arrest, His trial, His execution (described in detail) and His resurrection from the dead. All the preaching in the book of Acts drives to the cross (and the resurrection/reign of Jesus). Paul tells the Corinthians that he determined to 'know nothing while I was with you except Jesus Christ and him crucified' (1 Corinthians 2:2). Hebrews presents Jesus as our great High Priest who has gone not into the Jerusalem temple, but into heaven itself, bearing not animal blood, but His own blood, making a once-for-all atonement for sin. Peter calls slaves to follow the example of Jesus, based on the sacrificial death of the Servant in Isaiah 53 (1 Peter 2:21–25). John writes, 'This is love: not that we loved God, but that he loved us and sent his Son as an atoning sacrifice for our sins' (1 John 4:10). The book of Revelation shows the Lamb who was slain as the Lord of the universe. His blood purchased us for God (Revelation 5:9).

Salvation words

In *The Apostolic Preaching of the Cross*, Leon Morris traces the Old Testament classical and Jewish backgrounds for the New Testament words of salvation.[2] Here are his conclusions:

1. *Redemption:* To set free from slavery, with the payment of a substitutionary price. 'Instead of our death

there is His, instead of our slavery there is His blood . . .'

2. *Covenant:* God's unilateral agreement to bind Himself to us through the death of His Son. 'The new covenant is essentially a covenant based upon divine forgiveness of sin [through the blood of Jesus].'

3. *The blood:* Life poured out or given up in death. 'The blood which atones is that which flows when the death penalty is inflicted on the criminal [or the substitute who dies in his place].'

4. *Propitiation:* 'Where there is sin, there is wrath.' We cannot remove divine wrath by placating it. God does it by taking His own wrath upon Himself in the death of His Son.

5. *Reconciliation:* 'It is God's demand for holiness which causes the enmity [against mankind's sin].' God takes His enmity (wrath) upon Himself in His Son. The war is over; peace has come.

6. *Justification:* Christ, the righteous One, dies for the unrighteous, bearing their judgement in His death, so that we may be acquitted or justified before God by faith in Him. In the death of Christ, God proves Himself to be just (sin's penalty is paid) and the justifier of those who have faith in Jesus (Romans 3:26). 'Even the act of forgiveness which might be thought of as an act of mercy was seen to be also an act in accordance with righteousness. The very act wherein He delivers men is one in which He shows Himself to be acting righteously.' 'Righteousness . . . is a status conferred on men by God on the grounds of the atoning

work of Christ.' By faith, they will stand before Him 'not guilty' on the Day of Judgement.

The story of salvation

Tom Wright teaches us that the Exodus is 'the controlling narrative of the Bible'.[3] In Israel's deliverance two things happen. First, God's people are set free from slavery to Pharaoh and the gods of Egypt. Second, they are set free from the wrath of God. When the final plague, the death of the first born, falls on Egypt, Israel is subject to the same plague. But God provides a substitute. Each household is to sacrifice a lamb and mark the door with its blood. When the angel of death comes, seeing the blood, he passes over. Salvation then is to be delivered both from bondage and from the wrath of God.

When we fast-forward to the New Testament, we see that Jesus comes to bring the final Exodus. He sets us free, not from slavery to Egypt or Rome (or any other political power), but from slavery to Satan and his kingdom of darkness. Proclaiming the kingdom of God, He sweeps through Israel casting out demons and healing the sick. Then, as Paul says, Jesus disarms the demonic powers on the cross (Colossians 2:14–15). When He lifts the judgement of the law from us, He takes away Satan's power to accuse us and hold us in bondage.

Jesus also comes to set us free from the wrath of God against our sin. He is our Passover Lamb (1 Corinthians 5:7). His blood protects us. On the cross, He cries, 'My God, my God, why have you forsaken me?' (Mark 15:34).

As Helmut Thielicke says, 'In the cross there is a pain in God's heart.' The forsaken is also forgiving, pleading on our behalf: 'Father, forgive them, for they do not know what they are doing' (Luke 23:34). His death ends in triumph. Not 'I am finished' but 'It is finished' (John 19:30). The work of atonement is done. Divine justice is satisfied. God now forgives sinners freely through His Son.

Exploring all angles

Throughout their history, Christians have thought about the cross from a variety of perspectives. These are often called 'theories of the atonement'. It is better to call them 'angles on the atonement', because we will never understand fully what Christ has done for us on the cross. Each angle carries some truth. Here are three. First, there is the cosmic angle: on the cross Jesus defeated Satan. The devil thought he had killed God's Son, but, in a metaphor of the early church fathers, Jesus was the bait and the cross was the hook which reeled in our enemy. All the demonic power to afflict, infest, accuse and condemn is triumphed over in the cross (and in the resurrection of Jesus from the dead).

Second, there is the human angle. The cross reveals us. It scandalises us. It rips us apart. All self-justification dies here. We have executed the Son of God. 'When I survey the wondrous cross on which the Prince of Glory died, my richest gain I count but loss and pour contempt on all my pride.' But the cross reveals the depths of God's love at the same time. As we see Jesus' sacrifice, we are changed: 'Were the whole realm of nature mine, that were an offering far too small. Love so amazing, so divine, demands my soul, my life, my all.'

Third, more mysteriously, there is the divine angle. The cross is God's work for Himself before it is His work for us. In the cross He reconciles His justice and His mercy. As Luther says, holiness and love kiss in the cross. As Jesus dies in the place of sinners, divine justice is satisfied and divine mercy is extended. What changes is not God's heart to forgive us but the ground upon which He may do so (P. T. Forsyth).[4]

Conclusion

James Denney writes that if we were sitting on the end of a pier and a man came running down the pier crying, 'I love you, I love you,' and jumped into the swirling waters and was carried away, we would think him crazy. But if we were sitting on the end of a pier and fell into the swirling waters and were being carried away, and a man ran down the pier crying, 'I love you, I love you,' and jumped into the waters, throwing his arms around us and pulling us out, we would be eternally grateful. This is what Jesus has done for us as we are drowning in sin and judgement. Here is our debt to Him. We are eternally grateful and must express this at the heart of worship.[5]

In these times, it is so important that worship leaders and worship songwriters get to grips with the cross. It is the centrepiece of our faith, and as such we must explore every angle from which we can survey the wondrous, powerful cross.

the one thing...

Wayne Drain

I strongly encourage you to find a pastor or an older brother or sister in the Lord whom you can trust and be accountable to.

We are very privileged to do what we do as songwriters, artists or worship leaders. We often get much more attention than we either deserve or need. With this attention can come temptations such as pride or unfaithfulness. We need someone in our lives who will love and encourage us, but will not become so enamoured with us that they can't speak honestly into our lives. We need someone to ask us the hard questions about our character, as well as encouraging us in our giftings.

Accountability is not a four-letter word. It doesn't mean being controlled in an abusive manner. It means 'to be liable to be called to account'. It has to do with being responsible. Hebrews 13:17 says: 'Obey your leaders and submit to their authority. They keep watch over you as men who must give an account.' 'Obey' *is* a four-letter word, but it's a good one! It means 'to adapt to'. Accountability will help us adapt ourselves to the character of Christ as we seek to become more like Him in all we do.

The Real Worship Leader

Matt Redman

The Holy Spirit of God is the ultimate worship leader. In Philippians 3:3 we're reminded that we 'worship by the Spirit of God'. He is the agent and orchestrator of our worship. Nothing meaningful, spiritual or true happens in worship without Him. We become lead worshippers, setting an example for others to follow, while listening out for the essential promptings of the Holy Spirit.

There are some pretty big implications for us when we explore this view of the Holy Spirit as the worship leader. First, it relieves us of some pressure. When we see the Holy Spirit as the ultimate worship leader, we realise more than ever that we can't *make* worship happen. We can't hype it or conjure it up out of nowhere. Worship is always birthed by the Holy Spirit.

Yet at the same time this view keeps us dependent. We have a responsibility to make sure we're putting ourselves in the best possible place to hear those whisperings of the Holy Spirit. We are totally dependent on Him for the next step. I once heard Ken Gire use the analogy of a dance with the Lord. You don't necessarily have to know the end of the dance, you just have to follow His lead, step by step. Dependence is a vulnerable position, but as Oswald Chambers once said, 'Weakness and dependence will always be the occasion for the Spirit of God to manifest His power.'

In reality, no matter how many years' experience we have, we're just as dependent as the first time we ever led. We might be better singers now or know a few more chords – and these things are genuinely helpful – but the most vital factor hasn't changed at all: we need the Holy Spirit to help us lead, just as much as we ever did. He has no substitute or replacement. Formulas, experience, worship models and tried and tested songs will only take us so far. The Holy Spirit will always take us deeper.

If we take this view of worship leading, then before long we realise that not everything needs to originate from up the front. This has huge implications. We tend to get used to everything being led from the stage, but we must not assume that the Holy Spirit wants to lead the whole time of worship in song through only one person. Songs can start from within the congregation too. Scary, yes, but that is part of being dependent.

We'll even find ourselves praying before meetings differently too. Rather than just asking, 'Lord, anoint the musicians, the singers and the worship leader,' the priority prayer becomes, 'God, come and anoint Your people to worship You as we gather today.' A subtle shift, yet a momentous one.

There is of course real value in having a lead worshipper up the front – someone who's gifted in helping us travel together, and has thoughtfully prayed for some sense of direction – so there's no need to fire anybody. A slight change of approach is what's needed – more space to be led afresh by other members of the congregation, as they sense the Holy Spirit's leading.

Sometimes we get carried away, and forget that in the end the music is primarily just a tool (a beautiful tool, no question) to help us express our worship together. This shift of emphasis to see the Holy Spirit as Worship Leader strongly reminds us that we are involved here in a spiritual encounter, and not just a musical one.

Real worship will always be a spiritual event. So let us seek to follow the promptings of the real worship leader, the Holy Spirit.

the one thing...

Andrew Philip

We must learn to listen. First, to God, because He has spoken to us, and if we are to respond appropriately in worship we must make every effort to hear Him accurately. Second, to the world, because we are called to show mercy, and how are we to do that unless we hear its cries for help? And lastly, to one another in the church, because we all still carry our brokenness, and if we are to live in liberty we need to 'bear with one another in love'.

This is the context of our lives – the context in which we are living as we gather to worship. Our listening begins long before we pick up an instrument, and extends far deeper than merely trying to keep in time and play in the right key. Our listening – to God and to one another – forms the shape of our lives. And it is the shape of our lives that determines whether what we do when we gather on a Sunday morning is an expression of worship – something that truly brings God glory – or an expression of our selfishness, or disunity. God hears our hearts far more loudly than He does the sounds we make.

Skill and Sensitivity

Les Moir

I'd like to share about keeping your craft at a level that will allow you to flow with the Holy Spirit.

In the first few verses of Psalm 33 we're urged to make music to the Lord, sing to Him a new song and 'play skilfully'. The word 'skilfully' here means two things. First, we're to be the best on our instruments we can be – as practised and prepared as possible. And, second, we need to learn how to play sensitively, with an ability to flow with the Holy Spirit in our times of congregational worship. Musicians may have great technique, but without this sensitivity they will often distract from, rather than add to, the worship time. This sensitivity leads us to play the right thing at the right time. Apparently, Eric Clapton once said that his ambition was to make people cry by playing just one note! Sometimes less is actually more.

We also read in 1 Chronicles 25 about the Levite priests who took care of the worship in the temple, 'all of them trained and skilled in music for the Lord' (v. 7). We sense here a dedication to their calling, and so it should be with us. Whatever we do, we should work at it with all of our heart, spending time developing our gifting and learning to improve our playing as an expression of our love for Him. Take lessons, study, push yourself – learn different scales, chords and chord shapes – and learn to 'get into the groove with God'. Trumpet player and vocalist Phil Driscoll once commented, 'I am trying to keep my craft at a level that will allow me to flow with the Holy Spirit.'

As musicians, we can express the heart of God through our playing. Music is a language that God speaks through, just as He revealed in the rest of creation. The more we learn, the greater the vocabulary we'll have available to express what God is saying.

Be alert, as you never know where the Holy Spirit will lead. Let your worship be more than songs, but use the songs as a launch-pad into something new. For example, in times of intercession God may want you to express His heart for a nation with the sound of that culture, so learn to play other styles, or even indigenous instruments, and be ready.

In our times of worshipping as a team, it's great to express our worship to God together, but there may come a time and dynamic when you will feel prompted by the Holy Spirit to 'play out'. So spend time improvising, singing out new songs and making melody to God. And, remember, anything that can be spoken can be sung.

One weekend at a worship seminar I asked the musicians if they felt anything from the Lord. One of the bass players said he was feeling God's joy bubbling up. I handed him my bass and he started to play a funky bass figure. Soon the drummer and the whole band joined in and then everyone started to dance. Everyone there experienced the joy of the Lord in that moment.

I'm also reminded of being inspired by a violinist, Ruth Fazal, who would play out while Scripture was read aloud. She seemed to be able to convey the meaning of each verse as it was being read.

In the Old Testament, we see musicians being used to release the prophetic word. In 2 Kings 3:14 Elisha asks for a harpist to be brought, and while the harpist is playing, the hand of the Lord comes upon Elisha and he prophesies. We also see deliverance, as in the case of David playing before Saul. In 1 Samuel 16:23 we read that David would take his harp and play, then relief would come to Saul, and the evil spirit would leave him.

As musicians, we need to have one ear listening to the worship leader/musicians, and the other ear listening to what the Holy Spirit is saying and doing. Let's work at this, and learn to flow with the Holy Spirit.

the one thing...

Robin Mark

To thine own self be true. Be true to who you are and where you've come from. Be true to the culture and musical style that has been developed in your heart by God from all the unique exposure and experience you have lived.

Don't be embarrassed that your style might not be the 'in thing', for who really knows these things? Don't be fooled into thinking that if only you could emulate someone else's 'happening' style or apparently relevant creativity you would somehow touch a greater number of people.

The Bible is full of men and women whom God picked who didn't feel unique or special. They even told God that. Consider Moses: 'I can't speak right'; Gideon: 'I am the least of my brethren'; Isaiah: 'I am a man of unclean lips'; and even Abraham, who laughed at God (big mistake). And yet God decided they were the best people for the job. God used each of these people in all their unique weakness to accomplish amazing things for Him. Be true to yourself, and worship.

Understanding Worship: Part 2

Chris Jack

If we are serious about wanting to understand worship, we must look carefully at what the Bible says about it. The first step is to reflect on the words that lie behind the word 'worship'. The Bible of course was originally written in Hebrew (the Old Testament) and Greek (the New Testament). We begin, then, by looking at the relevant Hebrew and Greek words.

> There is a large vocabulary of words in Scripture that can contribute to our understanding of the whole theme or doctrine of worship. (David Peterson, *Engaging with God*, IVP, 1992, p. 17)

In the Old Testament there is an abundance of worship language. This language shows something of the variety and extent of Old Testament worship: its different forms and expressions, its personal and communal dimensions, its ordinary and extraordinary phenomena.

It all helps to inform us as to what worship is and how it should be offered.

There are three main Hebrew words used in the Old Testament for worship itself; that is, three words that are regularly translated in English versions by the word 'worship'. In short, the biblical terminology shows that worship is: submission, service, reverence. Significantly, all three have direct parallels in the Greek of the New Testament. What this means – and it is worth underlining at the outset – is that there is considerable consistency and continuity between the Old Testament understanding of worship and that of the New Testament. Certainly there are differences of content and form, but in terms of the basic understanding of what worship is and what it involves, there is a strongly unified picture that runs right through the Bible.

Each of these key words provides an important foundation for our understanding of what worship is. In point of fact, each conveys a different aspect of the complex, multifaceted activity we call worship.

> The biblical words for worship do not represent discrete concepts but are part of a whole mosaic of thought about the way to relate to God. They are important windows into that structure of thought. (David Peterson, *Engaging with God*, IVP, 2002)

The most common word for worship in the Old Testament is the Hebrew word *hawah*. The actual form found is *hishtahawah* and it means 'to bow (down)', 'to do obeisance', 'to pay homage' and, of course, 'to worship'. Of the 170 Old Testament occurrences of *hawah* just under half (approximately seventy-five) are translated 'worship' in the NIV. Around the same number are rendered 'bow down', with the simple 'bow' in several cases. In six passages the phrase 'pay honour' is used and in one 'pay homage'.

'Bowing (down)' is clearly a vital component of the meaning of the word. This physical gesture was common within the culture of the times. Bowing was a way of honouring someone, a mark of respect. It could also indicate submission, especially when performed in the presence of a figure of authority. Yet the important thing in all this is the intent behind the gesture. Of course, like any gesture, it could (and can) be performed superficially, even hypocritically. Action and attitude must go hand in hand. So, as a word for worship, *hawah* conveys the idea of honouring God and expressing an attitude of submission to Him.

We turn next to the Greek word *proskuneo*. Its meaning is well summarised by H. Schönweiss and C. Brown in *The New International Dictionary of New Testament Theology 2*:

> Among the Greeks the verb is a technical term for the adoration of the gods, meaning to fall down, prostrate oneself, adore on one's knees . . . In addition to the external act of prostrating oneself in worship, *proskuneo* can denote the corresponding inward attitude of reverence and humility. (p. 876)

Proskuneo is the most common word for worship in the New Testament (see, e.g., John 4:20–24; Revelation 5:14), just as *hawah* is in the Old Testament. Among other things, this enhances the sense of continuity between the two testaments. The primary idea behind the word is that of paying homage, honouring with a submissive spirit (and perhaps gesture) one who is deemed to be worthy and superior. As with *hawah*, it is essentially a matter of an inward attitude which may be reflected in an outward gesture. In both meaning and usage the two words, *hawah* and *proskuneo*, are extremely close parallels.

The unity of outlook between the New and the Old Testament is emphasised by the use of these parallel terms. This is important to grasp. In the core essentials of worship, the Old and New Testaments present a single, harmonious picture. There is a development between the Old and New Testaments in the area of forms and expressions of worship and, in particular, there is in the New Testament the momentous and unique revelation of Jesus Christ, with all its significance for worship. However, the essence of what worship is remains constant from Genesis to Revelation.

Looking at the first biblical word group, the parallel terms *hawah* and *proskuneo*, we are beginning to appreciate something of what the essence of worship is: worship involves humble submission to God.

The next biblical word group shows us that worship involves work or service. The relevant Hebrew term is *'abad*. In all, the word is found 289 times in the

Old Testament. Its range of meaning is 'to work', 'to do', 'to perform', 'to serve', 'to worship'. In the NIV it is most frequently translated by the word 'serve' (around 125 times). Quite often this is in contexts where God is the object of the verb, the One being served. The phrase 'to serve the Lord [Yahweh]' is used fifty-six times. It is in such usage that the notion of 'worship' is conveyed (see, e.g., Exodus 3:12; Deuteronomy 10:12; Isaiah 19:21), even where translators opt for 'serve' rather than 'worship'.

As well as being employed in a varied range of contexts where service of God is signified, *'abad* is also specifically used for religious service, including that related to the cult (sacrificial system, etc.) (e.g. Numbers 3:7f.; 8:11). The whole sacrificial system, with its detailed rituals and apparatus, was given by God to enable His people Israel to serve (worship) Him in an appropriate manner.

Moving on to the New Testament, there are two Greek verbs which, together with a number of related words, convey the same essential idea as *'abad*. They are *latreuo* and *leitourgeo*. *Latreuo* is found twenty-one times in the New Testament and means 'to serve', 'to worship'. It is translated in the NIV by 'worship' eight times, 'serve' twelve times and 'minister' once. All occurrences of *latreuo* are in religious contexts where the 'service' offered is not to another human being but to God (e.g. Luke 2:37; Acts 26:7; Philippians 3:3; Hebrews 12:28). Although in the Old Testament (Septuagint) the primary use of the word is in relation to the ceremonial worship of the sacrificial system, in the New Testament, other than in Hebrews, this becomes secondary.

The second Greek verb, *leitourgeo*, occurs only three times in the New Testament (Acts 13:2; Romans 15:27; Hebrews 10:11). Three other associated terms need to be noted: *leitourgia*, 'service', 'ministry' (six times); *leitourgikos*, 'serving', 'ministering' (once); and *leitourgos*, 'servant', 'minister' (five times).

In its range of meaning *leitourgeo* is very close to *latreuo*. However, its distinctive is that in the Septuagint (the Greek translation of the Hebrew Scriptures, produced in the second or third century BC) it is used almost exclusively for the service of priests and Levites in the temple. It effectively functions as a technical term for that service. In the New Testament usage of the word group this cultic association is preserved at times, particularly in Hebrews, where comparisons between the old covenant and the new are being made (Luke 1:23; Hebrews 9:21; 10:11). But at other times a non-cultic service is denoted (e.g. Philippians 2:25, 30).

Worship, then, is service of God expressed not only in religious gatherings, but in every area of life. It is worth reflecting on the fact that we refer to many of our meetings as 'services'. That is not inappropriate in the light of the insight received through this second biblical window onto worship. We might do well to ponder, however, how far our 'services' embody true 'service' of God!

We now complete our survey of the main biblical vocabulary for 'worship', looking through our third window to see that worship is 'fear' or 'reverence' of God.

The Hebrew word *yare'* is found over 300 times in the Old Testament. In the vast majority of instances it is translated in the NIV as 'afraid', 'fear' or some associated term. In approximately 80 per cent of the passages in which the verb is found, the object of fear is God. The concept of the fear of the Lord features strongly in the Old Testament, especially in the Wisdom books. Usually, such fear is not to be understood as 'terror' or 'dread', but as a heightened attitude of awe or respect.

On occasion, the NIV translates *yare'* as 'worship' – fifteen times in all (Judges 6:10; 1 Kings 18:12; 2 Kings 17:7, 25, 28, 32, 34, 35, 36, 37, 38, 39, 41; Isaiah 29:13; Jonah 1:9). By contrast, it is only so translated once in the RSV (Joshua 22:25). Interestingly, the one place where the RSV translators opt for 'worship', the NIV has 'fear'. Conversely, in 1 Kings 18:12 the RSV has 'revere' for the NIV's 'worship'. Note the flexibility of translation possibilities.

We may conclude that when used with reference to worship, *yare'* emphasises the idea of awe of or reverent respect for God.

> . . . worship as reverent obedience marked the practical out-working of the fear of God in the life of the community of faith – formally in proper religious service . . . and informally in right living. (Andrew Hill, *Enter His Courts with Praise*, Kingsway, 1998, p.4)

Andrew Hill rightly emphasises the implications of the attitude of fear or reverence of God in terms of obedience.

As the Old Testament Wisdom literature especially makes clear, 'the fear of the Lord' consists in a way of life that corresponds to the inner attitude of reverence towards God. And this way of life is itself an expression of worship. So worship is not just coming to God with a right attitude (reverence), but it is also the life(style) that issues from that attitude.

The New Testament equivalent of *yare'* is *sebomai*. It is used a number of times in the Septuagint for *yare'* (Job 1:9; Isaiah 29:13; Jonah 1:9). *Sebomai* occurs ten times in the New Testament. It means 'to revere', 'to worship', 'to be devout', and is translated as 'worship' six times in the NIV (Matthew 15:9; Mark 7:7; Acts 16:14; 18:7, 13; 19:27). Other occurrences are translated in the NIV as 'God-fearing' or 'devout' (Acts 13:43, 50; 17:4, 17). A number of related terms are found in the New Testament.

So, as with both word groups already studied, the New Testament once again confirms a perspective on worship first introduced in the Old Testament. This time it is that of worship as reverence of God: reverence that involves the dimension of awe. Our God is awesome! He is awesome in His greatness, His majesty and His holiness, to highlight a few key areas not always given their due place in our thinking and our worship today. Are the words of Tozer below, first preached forty years ago, perhaps even more true today?

I am finding that many Christians are really not comfortable with the holy attributes of God. In such cases I am forced to wonder about the quality of the worship they try to offer to him. (A.W. Tozer, 'Awed by the Presence of God', sermon preached in 1962)

There is one verse in the Old Testament which uses all three Hebrew words for worship that we have studied. The three windows onto worship – submission, service and reverence – are all brought together in a single verse: 2 Kings 17:35. It is interesting to compare how different translations handle this verse. The NIV reads: 'When the LORD made a covenant with the Israelites, he commanded them: "Do not worship [*yare'*] any other gods or bow down [*hawah*] to them, serve them [*'abad*] or sacrifice to them"' (2 Kings 17:35). In the RSV translation we read: 'The LORD made a covenant with them, and commanded them, "You shall not fear other gods or bow yourselves to them or serve them or sacrifice to them."'

In principle, each of the words could be translated 'worship': 'Do not worship . . . or worship . . . or worship . . .', though this would be rather flat and miss the nuances of the individual Hebrew words. Alternatively, as with the RSV, the choice could be made to translate none of the words as 'worship'. Either way, or however else the words are rendered into English, the verse is concerned with worship. True, in this instance it is the worship of 'other gods'; worship that the Lord insists should not be offered. But what is not to be offered to 'other gods' is to be offered to the one true God, as the next verse makes clear.

The important thing here is to understand that these

three – submission, service, reverence – are not alternatives representing three different forms of worship. Rather, they are three different facets of a single, complex activity, which is worship. So we begin to understand something of the nature of worship from a biblical perspective.

the one thing...

Rita Springer

Sometimes when we see worship being modelled with great music and a wonderful sound, we look at the talent and don't realise that true worship often comes with a price tag. We can tend to look for the end result and ignore the in-between stuff it takes to get us there.

Life brings us many circumstances and dreams, which sometimes come with a timetable and a box of patience. During those seasons, while we wait for release, we have a great opportunity to know Jesus more, and let Him be known through us.

Crafting Lyrics:
Songwriting: Part 2

Write about scriptural principles that are under-emphasised in contemporary worship songs. Try to use as much non-religious vocabulary as possible to paint a scripturally accurate picture of knowing and following God. Make sure the lyrics are more than just correct. They have to be compelling, and like a good sermon they have to appeal to the mind and emotions.

Make sure your lyrics are universal and they apply to all Christians. The various facets of relationship with God and our response to God's personality and commands are universal. Not only the content should be universal, but the vocabulary you are using should relate to a broad spectrum of people too. For example, avoid theological terms that will be unknown to some Christians and non-Christians. Instead, find creative ways, describing these terms in a fresh and personal way.

Andy Park

I am beginning to think that writing worship songs is far too important to leave to just the singers and musicians. For some reason, contemporary worship music seems to have unquestioningly taken on board the rock and pop model of the singer/songwriter, and so assumes that the singer/musician should be the one to write both the words and the music of the song. Why?

I know we have some great songs around, but let's not be too easily satisfied. We need to get the theologians involved with poets and the lyricists, and get them all involved with the music writers. We mustn't be 'precious' about all this.

Andy Piercy

Jesus says, 'Out of the overflow of the heart the mouth speaks' (Matthew 12:34). The heart is the main wellspring for lyrics. If what goes in is rich, the fruit is likely to be rich. If what we are feeding on is shallow, our lyrics will become dry and uninspiring. We need to overflow from the word of God. There is no substitute for the revelation God brings through His written word.

Be ruthless with your lyrics. Don't settle for lines that are second best. When it comes to putting song lyrics together it is good to try and say things in a fresh way, avoiding over-done rhymes such as 'You pour out Your grace, as I seek Your face'. The real skill is putting an old theme in a fresh and inspiring way.

Martyn Layzell

Songwriters are philosophers and should take their art and ministry seriously. What is written is pondered by the mind and many times received in the heart, affecting the listener in the deep places of their heart. Music combined with lyrics is a powerful force because you contemplate it and say it over and over.

We have a responsibility because of this to be God-centred and theologically sound. Songs are miniature injections into people or groups, so desire your injection to honour God.

Charlie Hall

The congregational lyric-writer must have a pastoral heart. They need not necessarily be the greatest counsellor or the ultimate listening ear, but they must have a heart for the people of God. With every line of the song, let's remember our congregations. Never honour the music above the people. In other words, make every effort to write singable songs. In the same way, go out of your way to write lyrics that are easy for the congregation to understand and make their own. Too many times I've seen worship song lyrics that are so subjective and particular to the writers that no one singing them actually has a clue what they're saying, and all this done in the name of poetry. But people are more important than poetry. By all means be a poet, but first of all be a pastor.

Matt Redman

I think that writing congregational song lyrics is something we don't labour over as much as we should. It is very easy to write obvious lyrics, using the classic clichés, but to write something fresh that really adds to a church's worship takes time and thought.

When writing a worship song I always turn to the Bible to see what it says on the matter. But I've been trying to get beyond just simply copying down verses from the Bible and putting them into songs. Though that is a valid way to write scripture songs, there's also something to be said for trying poetically to express these timeless truths in different ways. Some songs are even a mixture of many different parts of Scripture.

Lastly, we need to keep finding ways of expressing God's majesty and glory. Do our lyrics open eyes up to the greatness of God? Do they fill our minds and hearts with the glorious truth of who He is? They are the songs the church needs to sing.

Tim Hughes

the one thing...

Tommy Walker

May the dream never die that some day, when people want to go and find the most moving and excellent art, they will go to the church. I am so convinced that we've only just begun to tap into some of the improvisational sounds that can be created in the presence of God. These are the sounds the world can't touch, yet will be drawn to.

Cell, Congregation, Celebration

Matt Redman

Jesse Owens, Carl Lewis, Michael Johnson: some of
the greatest athletes ever known. But what makes
them so remarkable? What distinguishes them from other
great athletes of their time? In a word, their 'versatility'.
Countless athletes over the years have had victories in
one track event or another. But much rarer is an athlete
who can tackle more than one distance and make it their
own. The 100 metres, for example, is a totally different
event from the 400 metres. And somewhere in between
lies the discipline of the 200 metres. All involve running,
but they're completely different races. Each needs a different approach, and a different pace.

It's the same with worship leading. And again, 'versatility' is the key word. Some of us may be able to lead in a
cell/home group setting, but how good are we at adapting
ourselves to leading a congregation (i.e. lots of cell/home
groups joined together)? Some of us may be called to lead
in a celebration-type meeting (in other words, a worship

gathering of more than one congregation), but what different approach is needed for that? Whether we're leading worship in a cell, a congregation or a celebration, there are certain key values and principles that they all have in common. Yet in another way they're totally different 'races', and each one requires a slightly different approach.

So which of these three settings is the hardest to lead worship in? I've thought about this for a while and come to the conclusion that they are all about the same. There's not really one setting in which it is harder to lead. Each group has its own advantages, but also comes with a specific set of challenges for you to get your head around as the worship leader.

Cell

You can't beat the cell group for that intimate, raw, community vibe. If you can get it right, there's something special about singing out to God in someone's front room, with little more than an acoustic guitar. It feels so uncomplicated, so free of distractions and so 'New Testament' (apart from the acoustic guitar, of course). If we can lead people to 'the secret place of praise' in this small setting, it can be a beautiful thing.

The first step is to help people realise that what we're doing goes way beyond this little room; that when we lift our voices together (however weak or thin that may sound) we reach way beyond the confines of this room and touch heaven. Maybe we get this sense across by the way we introduce our worship, or maybe through what we pray at the beginning, but however we do it, this is an essential key to unlocking a meaningful time of worship in this environment. In the down-to-earth setting of a home group, it's so important to prepare our hearts for a 'spiritual' event. Once that happens, suddenly no one is focusing on what their neighbour's voice sounds like, or if their own voice is in tune. We become caught up with the living God.

One of the biggest challenges of leading in this setting is that it feels so vulnerable. There is no band to hide behind, and not even the 'security blanket' of a microphone. It's important that we sing out confidently, as this creates an environment where other people are likely to feel freer to sing their hearts out too. Sing loudly enough so that people can hear you to follow, but not so loudly that you become a distraction. Build up a vocabulary of songs – partly so you don't have the complication of turning pages every other minute, but also so you can flow spontaneously with a new idea at any moment. Practise tempos to songs because songs can very easily drag in a setting where there's no band to fill in the gaps.

Once you've got beyond some of these initial practicalities, the biggest challenge in a cell group setting is to keep it fresh. This is a challenge when leading regularly in any worship setting, but in a cell group it's even more acute, because you generally have fewer songs to choose from. If you take a list of all the songs you sing on a Sunday morning in the congregation, so many of these aren't appropriate or attainable when it comes to the home group setting. Some songs have notes that are too high. You can belt them out when there are 200+ of you and a rousing band to accompany the anthem, but when it comes to five of you in your front room, with nothing but a lone acoustic guitar, things are a little more, shall we say, 'exposed'. Other songs get ruled out because they have male and female repeat lines. In reality, most home groups (unless you have a particularly strong and confident group of singers) can't cope with that.

The most common reason why songs don't make the transition from congregation to cell is that they're too 'wordy'. It's simply not feasible for the average person to memorise a load of lengthy songs that they get to sing now and again at the weekend. I guess in theory you could have an overhead projector set up, or word sheets (if you've covered the copyright aspects), but this somehow jars with the raw, uncomplicated and intimate environment that is a home group.

For me, the key is to work with sections of these songs. Maybe the chorus is instantly memorised, and stands up well on its own. Or maybe you could take just one, easily learned, verse from a hymn and segue into it at an appropriate moment when you're ending another song. You could even take just one particularly repeatable line from a song, and tag it onto the end of another song, just to bring some freshness. Finally, you might want to take an up-tempo song, bring it down a few keys, and use it as a slower, more tender, offering. Again, it can breathe a fresh lease of life into an old song, and help keep you fresh in your worship leading.

The beauty of the cell setting is that there's room to be spontaneous. The overhead projector operator doesn't need a list of songs (because there isn't an overhead projector operator), and you don't need to worry whether the band know a song or not (because there isn't a band). In a sense, leading worship in a cell group is like driving a little speedboat – it's easy to make various twists and turns, whether they're planned or not. When it comes to the congregation/celebration settings, you're captaining a very different ship – more comparable to a big tanker – and it takes more thought, effort and experience in order to make unexpected turns.

Congregation

That's not to say spontaneity is impossible in the congregation (and celebration) setting. It just has to be a little more rehearsed (however contradictory that sounds). In other words, you need to train your musicians (and overhead projector operator) to be able to flow with the spontaneous. Make space in practice times to flow together spontaneously: try running songs into one another 'seamlessly'; try different endings; try playing songs in various keys so you can adapt them to link with different songs. Create a team that respects the discipline of a well-rehearsed song, yet is ready and able to flow with any changes of direction and approach that seem appropriate.

In reality, it's a huge step to go from leading worship in a cell group to leading in a congregational setting. The number of practical things you need to consider doubles.

Anyone can play in time with themselves (well, nearly anyone!), but leading a band is a completely different matter. Practise starting and ending songs cleanly. Find some subtle hand signals (that don't resemble rude gestures!) with which to direct the band during unplanned moments. Make sure both you and your musicians/singers memorise as many songs as possible so you can pay maximum attention to flowing together musically, joining with the congregation and, most of all, fixing your eyes on Jesus.

Working as part of a team is probably the biggest difference after leading alone in a small group. There are so many people to connect with and learn to flow with: the speaker, the band, the sound engineer, the congregation and, of course, the pastor. (Remember that the pastor is in authority and if you do not get affirmation from your pastor on the matter, don't turn your amp up to 10!) When you arrive at church to lead worship, remember that you are coming to serve, and not to be served. That will have a hugely positive bearing on your relationships with all of the above people, and ease you through a whole host of tensions that could otherwise build up.

When you lead in a cell group, it's quite likely that you're all a similar age and, to some degree, the same sort of people. There's a good chance you even all like the same kinds of music. But when you come into the congregational setting, it's a different picture. There will most probably be lots of different age groups, and types of people, with different preferred songs, styles and sounds. Again, the key is servant leadership. Find an appropriate volume for the band which will not alienate or offend. Don't just choose songs from your own personal preferences, but begin to find out which songs are the most helpful to various groups in terms of leading them into worship.

As well as presenting a challenge, this issue of leading lots of different ages and types of people at one time is an amazing blessing. How many other places on earth do you find so many different voices singing one song? If you can foster that sense of the family of God, worshipping with one voice, it is an incredibly powerful thing.

Celebration

Whereas the congregation feels like a great big family gathered to worship God, the celebration setting tends to carry more the sense of a great big army. It is an amazing experience to be among many hundreds (or thousands) of worshippers, gathered from over a wider area.

Having said that, beware the allure of 'big' things. In kingdom terms, bigger does not necessarily mean better. For sure, a big meeting can provide a most incredible encounter with the almighty God. But if it is to be truly meaningful, we need to approach leading the meeting with a purity of heart and a focus on what we are doing.

Lesson number one for me is always that a great band does not automatically equal great worship. In these settings there are often more musicians and singers for us to choose from, so in reality we may end up with a pretty decent band. Wonderful – as long as we don't end up losing our dependence on God. Too many times I've been tricked into thinking, 'Great band, great sound system, lots of people. Wow, it's going to be a great night of worship.' As soon as you catch yourself descending into this sort of thought pattern, repent and get back on track. It's essential that we stay in the place of complete dependence. Great music alone cannot usher in great worship. We must look to the Holy Spirit's promptings, and be as dependent on Him as we were the very first time we ever stood up to lead.

Again, keep an eye on the practical things that present themselves in this situation. The band needs to be loud enough so that people can 'travel together', yet not so loud they can't hear themselves sing. Be ready to sing some songs without the instruments. Don't fall into the trap of thinking you need to use the band on every single song just because they are there.

Out of the three worship settings we've looked at, this is the one where it's most likely not everyone will know the same songs. That's definitely a big consideration. It's important to make sure that somewhere in the mix of songs are ones that every church-going person in the room is likely to know. Again, it's all about travelling together. It's a terrible shame if people return home having never really lifted up their many voices together as 'one choir'.

If we can get it right in this situation, it opens up our eyes of faith in an amazing way. Joining together like this is powerful in itself, yet deep inside we know that what we are seeing is a mere glimpse of the day when every tribe and every tongue will gather together to sing the great praises of Jesus.

Let's be versatile as lead worshippers. In every situation let's learn to lead with pastoral wisdom, creative insights and sensitivity to the Holy Spirit's every whisper.

the one thing...

Charlie Groves

The one thing I'd say to musicians and those involved in leading worship is 'Keep going!' It's essential to take the long view when getting actively involved in God's church. To those outside, being a worship leader or in the band can seem like the place for those who've really made it and everyone just surfs along on a spiritual high! That's not always the case. Sometimes it feels like being in the front line of the battle – worship is a highly contested area (see Ephesians 6:12). Sometimes private anxieties, self-doubt and accusations seem to arrive from just about every angle. Combine that with the fact that we musicians can be pretty sensitive by nature, and it's not always the easiest place to be.

Many of us have had moments when we felt like throwing in the towel and advertising our guitar in the local newspaper. But, like Paul, we've got to run the race. We need to 'throw off everything that hinders . . . and run with perseverance the race marked out for us'

(Hebrews 12:1–3). It helps to have a sure knowledge that God has called us to do this work. Confidence in our calling will help to sustain us through the difficult times.

Keep praying, keep rejoicing, keep being a team player, keep serving the people . . . keep going!

Praise the Lord! (A Commentary on Psalm 150)

Don Williams

The final shout of the Psalter is the imperative 'Praise the Lord!' Throughout this vast body of literature, we are called to this again and again. The study of the Psalms would be a futile exercise if we failed to hear and heed this exhortation. The greatest truth of God is that He is worthy of our worship, and the deepest truth about ourselves is that we have been created to worship Him. When we actually do this, we find the real and eternal end, or *telos,* of our existence. Why is it that so many people are hard, cold, loveless, fearful, introverted, sad, scared, empty, angry, violent, cunning, self-centred, self-consumed? The bottom line answer is that they have never really worshipped God. They have never bowed to Him, submitted to Him, seen Him in His glory and love, and risen up to praise Him, to make joyful noises and shouts before Him. They have never known this release, or if they have known it for a moment, they have re-fused to stay there, wedded to worship, dwelling in the presence and receiving the power of Almighty God granted to us through His Son in His Spirit.

As the end of this age draws near, the issues are increasingly clear. The battle lines are drawn. We either worship the living God, or we worship the devil with all his masks and disguises. But how shall we worship? Where will we learn to worship Him? The first answer is biblical. The Psalms will teach us and reform our worship, if we will hear them. They will lead us to God-centred worship rather than human-centred aesthetics or theatrics. They will teach us that worship is surrender to the great King who reigns, and we will make that surrender. They will show us how to praise Him, recounting His character and His works, which make Him worthy of our praise and evoke our joy. We will also learn to wait upon Him, to sit in the silence, to listen for His voice. We will grow in the expectancy that we will hear His living word addressed to us. We will also learn to petition Him as our King, and expect to receive His answers and see Him prove that He is the living God who is active in our midst once again. We will expect to see His salvation, healing, deliverance, peace and comfort as we hear His word and see His work. All of this will result in greater and greater surges of praise ascending to His throne, until that day when we are caught up to be with Him for ever.

Psalm 150 (NRSV) ends the Psalter with a call to praise. The word 'praise' is repeated thirteen times in six verses. This psalm is a little introduction to and summary of what real worship is: expressing joyful delight in the presence of God.

Praise the Lord!
Praise God in His sanctuary;
Praise Him in His mighty firmament!

Verse 1 opens with the common exhortation: 'Praise the Lord!' Written in the plural, it addresses all of us together. It answers the question of *what* we are to do when we come into the presence of the mighty King. We come offering Him our cries and shouts of glory to His name. We come expressing our love, our delight and our adoration to Him. But where are we to do this?

First, we are to praise God 'in His sanctuary'. This, of course, is His temple or palace in Jerusalem. Down through the generations, the Jews went up to Jerusalem to worship the Lord as long as the temple stood. With the coming of Jesus, however, the veil of the temple, which separated the people from the holy presence of God, was removed, and the temple itself was later destroyed in judgement. Now we worship God through the temple of the risen body of Jesus Himself (John 2:13ff.), and as believers we are all incorporated into that body. Also our individual bodies (in reflection of His) have become little temples where God chooses to dwell by His Spirit (1 Corinthians 6:19). Today, as we gather in corporate worship, we are the living temple of God, and we are the body of Christ in ministry together.

We also worship God 'in His mighty firmament'. He is to be worshipped across the vast expanse of heaven. Heaven and earth are to join together and become one in praising Him (see Psalm 148). Verse 2 of Psalm 150 continues:

Praise Him for His mighty acts;
Praise Him according to His excellent greatness!

What is our motive as we come into the presence of the Lord to praise Him? First, we are to 'praise Him for His mighty acts'. To do this we must remember the great things He has done in creation and history. His acts reveal His character. Through them we learn of the Creator's majesty. Through them we learn of His awesome righteousness and justice as He pounds Egypt with plagues and tears down the walls of Jerusalem. And through them we learn of His love and mercy, His covenant treaty with us, His faithfulness towards us, consummated in the new covenant in His Son's blood.

We must also remember His mighty acts in our own lives. He provides for us day by day. He enters our lives through His Spirit. He answers our prayers. He delivers us from our enemies. He heals our diseases. He unites us to each other in love. He matures us in His word. He employs us in His kingdom work, and He remains faithful. Indeed, 'Praise Him for His mighty acts'.

We are also to 'praise Him for His excellent greatness' (literally, 'the multitude of His greatness'). God is great; He is full of 'greatness'. No one is greater than He. We praise Him for who He is, not only for what He has done. He is the mighty King. He is the eternal God. He is the source of all things; all things come from Him and return to Him. He is filled with holiness, justice, trustworthiness and covenant love. He is the alpha and the omega; the beginning and the end. Worship this great

God. Our motives for praise are twofold. We praise God for what He has done, and we praise Him for who He is. But how are we to praise His name?

Praise Him with the sound of the trumpet;
Praise Him with the lute and harp!
Praise Him with the timbrel and dance;
Praise Him with stringed instruments and flutes!
Praise Him with loud cymbals;
Praise Him with clashing cymbals!
Let everything that has breath praise the Lord.
Praise the Lord!

The psalmist offers us the means of our praise as he describes the ancient musical instruments of Israel. God is to be praised with the 'sound of the trumpet' (the ram's horn, used for signalling), the 'lute' (a several-stringed instrument with a sound chamber), the 'harp', the 'timbrel' (a woman's instrument used in dance), 'stringed instruments', 'flutes', 'loud cymbals', and 'clashing cymbals' (types of percussion instrument). God is to be praised by a symphony of sound (vv. 3–5). Today we may legitimately add our own musical instruments to the list. Everything that evokes or expresses praise is a legitimate instrument of praise and therefore relevant for the culture using it. The issue is not what instruments we use; the issue is why we use them and how we use them.

Our voices lifted in praise are to be accompanied by instruments of praise. We are also to 'dance' (v. 4). Physical expressions in worship are important. The real issues are whether such dance comes from the heart, is Spirit-led (rather than for show) and is appropriate to the gathering. Ask whether it is presented as an offering to Almighty God.

As this psalm and the Psalter concludes, there is a final exhortation, which refers us back to verse 1: 'Let everything that has breath praise the Lord.' The animals have breath; they are to praise the Lord. The birds have breath; they are to praise the Lord. Humans have breath; they are to praise the Lord. This is the purpose of breath, the spirit (*ruach*) that God breathed into us (Genesis 2:7). We are to breathe it back to Him in praise as we offer the essence of our life up to Him. Indeed, as the psalm ends, 'Praise the Lord!'

the one thing...

Graham Ord

I often think about worship leading as pastoring people through music. Our music helps people to meet with Jesus and in turn we are expectant that Jesus will meet with them. In this way worship leading takes on a pastoral role.

People are very precious. Through loving them, we are kept in touch with the fragile nature of life, and also with our desperate need of God. Compassion curbs our tendencies towards selfishness. By developing pastoral hearts we gain the sensitivity we vitally need to lead people before the One who is 'more than enough' for them. We should always stay profoundly aware that our music in itself is actually powerless to save anyone.

What Bands Want from Their Worship Leaders

Matt Weeks

Worship leading is mostly looked at through the lens of how the lead worshipper relates to the congregation; and rightly so. Yet there is another dynamic at play: you've got to lead your band too. So what do bands want from their leaders?

First, confidence. A band will respond much better when the worship leader exudes a certain amount of confidence. Not arrogance in any respect, but a humble confidence – the sense that they know where they are heading, and know how to get there.

Second, communication. Once a vision or direction has been decided, the worship leader must communicate this clearly to the band. Most musicians will respond to your confidence enthusiastically, but it may not necessarily be in the exact way that you meant them to respond. Remember: always over-communicate rather than under-communicate.

Third, encouragement. If you've started to communicate to your players and singers, your feedback on how they are doing is extremely vital. Whether you need to clarify something, or just say that it was exactly right, your encouragement to them is so important. This applies not only to musical activity but to spiritual activity too.

A worship leader's role contains a combination of musical and pastoral aspects. A band will look for maturity in both areas from their worship leader. Musical maturity will help you to understand where your band members are coming from, from their musical preferences right down to the suggestions they make during rehearsal times. It will also give your team more confidence in the decisions you make. So aim to learn a little more about the theories and techniques behind what you do, and broaden your listening vocabulary too. Pastoral maturity is important because musicians can be tender and fragile souls. They often make themselves vulnerable by putting their heart into expressing something that could be torn down or easily ignored. Aim to be approachable and encouraging.

It's well worth being aware of the different types of musician that may be a part of your team. In very broad terms there are two types of musician, and most members of your worship team will fit somewhere along the spectrum of these two extremes. At one end you have the less experienced and less confident player or singer, and at the other end you find the experienced, confident player or singer.

All musicians will benefit from encouragement, whether they are beginners or seasoned performers. Less experienced, unsure players may want you to encourage them by taking them under your wing, whereas the more experienced player is more likely to want to be encouraged in a way that gives them wings and releases them. Whatever level a musician or singer is at, tell them if they've got it right! So often a worship leader will point out things that are wrong or need to be altered, but if they aren't told what is good too, they may never quite be sure if what they are playing is appropriate. Be as verbal about the things that are right as you are about the things that are wrong.

Lastly, environment is everything. Try to create an atmosphere in which your musicians and singers feel safe, and are free to be creative. Given space to experiment, a band will grow in skill, confidence and unity.

the one thing...

Tom Lane

What has helped me the most as a leader in worship is honesty. Since God already knows what's in my heart I obviously can't fool or impress Him, so I've learned to be real with Him. Every time I get up to lead people, I am totally aware of how very little I have to offer Him in the way of assistance.

creative insight

Worship and Justice –
An Interview with Mike Pilavachi

What is the link between worship and justice?

There are many ways to live out our worship, and pursuing God's heart of justice for the poor and the broken is one of them. Worship and justice are two sides of the same coin, and they're inextricably linked.

A key scripture that's challenged me is Amos 5:23–24. These verses say, 'Away with the noise of your songs! I will not listen to the music of your harps. But let justice roll on like a river, and righteousness like a never-failing stream!' Here you get a sense of God's anger and broken heart at a people who may have sung all the right songs and done all the right things in the temple, and yet whose lives were not matching up. They weren't living out God's justice. They failed to see that actually to care for the poor, the broken, the oppressed and those on the margins of society is an important aspect of worship.

So where does that leave us in terms of singing our worship songs?

We don't want to downplay the role of singing songs, or reject what we do in the gathered community. And we certainly don't want to downplay adoration. But to simply gaze into the eyes of our heavenly Father while we look with contempt on the poor, the broken and the despised is a contradiction in terms.

John says in his first letter: 'If anyone says, "I love God," yet hates his brother, he is a liar. For anyone who does not love his brother, whom he has seen, cannot love God, whom he has not seen' (1 John 4:20). In a sense it's as simple as that. It's reconnecting what we do when we sing, with the whole of our lives.

In Matthew 25 Jesus says to the righteous, 'The King will say . . . "I was hungry and you gave me something to eat, I was thirsty and you gave me something to drink . . . I needed clothes and you clothed me"' etc. The righteous will say, 'When did we see you hungry . . . ?' And the King will reply, '. . . whatever you did for one of the least of these brothers of mine, you did for me.' Jesus is explicitly saying that how we treat the poor and the outcasts of society is inextricably linked with what we offer Him. When we really live out a life of worship it makes what we do when we sing so much more meaningful.

Some people would argue that if we are to live lives caring for the poor, why waste time and money in improving the quality of music, or in PA systems, when that money could be given to the poor. What would you say to that?

That was exactly what was said to Mary Magdalene when she broke the alabaster jar of perfume all over Jesus' feet; perfume that was worth over a year's wages. We see in John 12 that she poured it over Jesus and it was extravagant and it was wasteful. The question was asked, 'Why wasn't this perfume sold and the money given to the poor?' Jesus' response was, 'You will always have the poor among you, but you will not always have me.'

The Lord called Israel to give of their best for the temple, and bring sacrifices to God. When we do that, there will always be more than enough left over to give to the poor. It's when we have a poverty mentality to God that somehow we find we don't have enough resources to give to the poor.

If we're not extravagant in our worship of Jesus then we're actually nothing more than glorified social workers.

So how do we work this out practically in our everyday lives?

We try to find all sorts of ways to flesh out our pursuit of worship and justice. On a Sunday we have a black plastic bin at the front of church. Someone once said that a church's architecture reflects its theology. So if a church has a big altar table and candles you know it has a certain theology. If there's a big pulpit with a brass eagle staring down, you say that the church has a certain theology. Well, we have this black bin at the front of our church and during the offering, when people tithe their money to the Lord's work, we also bring food and other items. These are given to the social services, who distribute them to people in need. It's symbolic. This big black bin reminds us as we worship that we must always remember the poor.

The most interesting thing for me, as the pastor, is that the people most active in ministering to the broken seem to be the ones most engaged in worship on a Sunday too. It's not either/or. It's two sides of the same coin. I know for me that the more I grow to love Jesus the more I end up having His compassion for a broken and hurting world.

We must worship God with adoration, praise and thanksgiving in the 'temple', then from that place go out in power to live a life that's pleasing to Him.

the one thing...

Nigel Morris

Our worship of Jesus is always a response to who He is, or rather how we perceive Him to be. If He is somewhat small in our hearts and minds, our response may remain minimal, mechanical and even miserly. But as we see Him more and more for who He really is, realising what He has done for us, then pouring out our lives and resources will be our joyful response and our heart's desire.

Understanding Worship: Part 3
Chris Jack

Forms of worship in the Old Testament

'**W**orship is not a recent invention.' So Derek Tidball reminds us in his brief study of worship in *On the Bridge* (Baptist Union, 1992). The roots of Christian worship reach back well over 2,000 years, to the Old Testament era. Indeed, we cannot properly understand New Testament teaching about worship without an appreciation of worship in the Old.

> For many Christians, the Old Testament remains a mysterious and seemingly irrelevant book. At no point does it appear more distant from the needs and aspirations of people in secularised cultures than when it focuses on the temple, the sacrificial system and the priesthood. Yet these institutions were at the very heart of ancient thinking about worship and their significance must be grasped if New Testament teaching is to be properly understood. (David Peterson, *Engaging with God*, IVP, 2002, p. 23)

This is why we begin with the Old Testament, despite the fact that its worship looks so different from what we are familiar with as Christians. I can't recall ever attending a Sunday service at which a bull or a lamb was offered as a burnt offering, yet we'll see that although Christian worship is very different in many of its particulars from Old Testament worship, patterns and values found there are foundational for Christian worship today.

We are talking of Old Testament worship as if it were a single, uniform entity. Yet the first thing we must note is that within the Old Testament there is considerable diversity in terms of the forms used to express worship. The Old Testament is of course a sizeable body of literature. Its thirty-nine books were written over a lengthy period of time and span several millennia of history at least. During this time, from the patriarchs to the post-exilic era, worship was by no means static. It underwent change. It developed. This development is essentially due on the one hand to God's continuing (progressive) revelation of Himself and of His requirements for His people, and on the other to the changing circumstances and contexts in which God's people found themselves.

An example of this, focusing on the 'locus' of worship (the place(s) where worship regularly took place), is found in the table following.

Developments in
Old Testament Worship

Patriarchal Period	*Sacred places*
Exodus – settlement in Canaan	*Tabernacle*
Monarchy	*Temple*
Exile	*Synagogues*
Restoration	*Second temple*

Behind the apparently simple matter of where people worshipped stands a whole range of associated issues which reflect something of the variety and diversity of Old Testament worship practices, as we shall see.

During the patriarchal period (the stories of Abraham, Isaac, Jacob and Joseph, told in Genesis) worship was largely informal. A reading of the stories narrated reveals that often no formal requirements for worship are set out; there are no set patterns of worship; there is no absolute requirement to offer sacrifices; there are no set rituals for offering sacrifices when such are part of the worship; there is no fixed location, either in terms of a temple or a fixed shrine; there is no established priesthood. It is true that on occasion some directions are given (e.g. Genesis 15:9f.), but these are related to a specific act of worship rather than representing the establishing of norms. Here, sacrifice is a common, though not essential, element of worship (e.g. Genesis 28, Jacob at Bethel).

Worship can be offered anywhere; it is not restricted to set locations. However, certain locations do take on particular significance by association with an encounter with

God that has taken place there. Altars are erected, which become sacred places especially appropriate for offering sacrifice and for further meetings with God (e.g. Genesis 35:1–14). Nevertheless, these sacred places never become the exclusive worship sites; there is always the possibility of a significant encounter with God at a new location, which then becomes a new sacred place. God is not bound to any one location or group of sites.

Patriarchal worship is spontaneous, involving response to a particular revelation of God or to some intervention of His on behalf of the worshipper(s). It is generally an individual response, or that of a family, so it is intensely personal.

[Patriarchal worship] is divinely initiated and motivated . . . The worship of God only occurs as he chooses to reveal aspects of his divine purpose and character to human beings through word and deed . . . the worship of God is a response to this divine self-disclosure. (Andrew Hill, *Enter His Courts with Praise*, Baker Book House, 1997, pp. 31f.)

So the pattern of worship that emerges during the patriarchal era in the book of Genesis is one that is informal, flexible, spontaneous and personal. It is always a response to God's initiative.

Although the external form of worship undergoes significant changes during the exodus period, the worship offered is no less conditioned by God's initiative. It is in fact a response to God's momentous act of deliverance, the exodus. For the Israelites this was the greatest single initiative God (Yahweh) ever took on their behalf, perpetually commemorated in the feast of the Passover. Of course, the Passover, as well as being a time of remembrance, is also a significant act of worship.

The exodus, God's redemptive act by which the Israelites were gloriously delivered from slavery in Egypt (Exodus 1–15), is the defining event in Israel's history. It's an event often referred to in later times (over 120 references in the Old Testament). Through the exodus, and the subsequent encounter with God at Sinai (Exodus 19ff.), Israel was established as the people of God. The basis of this unique relationship is the covenant God makes with His people (see, e.g., Exodus 19:1–8). The terms of the covenant are set out in the Law God gives them there.

A further provision of God at Sinai was the cult (or cultus). This is the short-hand term used to encompass all that is involved in the formal worship centred on the Tabernacle (and, later, the Temple), with its system of sacrifices, its priesthood, its rituals and its sacred objects. In the context of the giving of the Law and the detailed instructions concerning the construction of the Tabernacle and the worship to be conducted there, a fundamental worship principle is highlighted: that of obedience to God.

> . . . absolute obedience to God the Creator and Redeemer is required as the basic necessary attitude of the people who truly worship God. (Yoshiaki Hattori)

At Sinai God laid down for His people the actual forms

in which worship should be expressed. And central to this was sacrifice. Sacrifice played a central role in the corporate worship of Israel. Furthermore, there was just one official sanctuary where sacrifice was to be offered: the Tabernacle. (For details see Exodus 25–31 and 35–40; also the book of Leviticus.)

So, once again, worship is seen to be a response to God's initiative. More than that, it is now also a response to His specific directives. He tells His people precisely *how* they are to worship Him. This is a clear development from the much more informal worship offered in the patriarchal era.

The Tabernacle was a portable sanctuary. In time, once the Israelites were settled in the land of Canaan, the promised land, the Tabernacle was replaced by the Temple. The latter, built by King Solomon, was a more permanent sanctuary, located in Jerusalem. Once the Temple had been completed (1 Kings 5–7; 2 Chronicles 2–4), the ark of the covenant, which symbolised the very presence of God, was transferred to it and the Temple was dedicated (1 Kings 8; 2 Chronicles 5–7). The description of the accompanying phenomena of cloud and fire (2 Chronicles 5:13f.; 7:1f.), associated in the text with the glory of God, has strong parallels with the account following the completion of the Tabernacle in Exodus 40:34–38. These parallels confirm the legitimacy of the Temple as the new sanctuary.

In practice, other than a tendency towards elaboration in the ceremonial associated with the rituals, undoubtedly fostered by the sheer grandeur of the new surroundings, little changed. Temple worship was essentially a continuation of Tabernacle worship.

The cataclysmic events of the exile, with the destruction of Jerusalem and its Temple, together with the deportation of many of its inhabitants, brought enforced changes to Israel's worship. With no recognised sanctuary, no cult, no focal meeting place, the Jews had to adapt. They did so by giving a central role to the Torah, the Law, as enshrined in their Scriptures. They became increasingly a people of the book. Although the origins of the synagogue (such a prominent feature in the Gospels) are far from clear, it is widely held that it was during the exile that they came into being. These were not mini-temples, for no cult was practised there. Rather, they were meeting places where the faithful gathered to pray and to read the Torah.

Following the exile, when Jews returned to Jerusalem (the Restoration), the Temple was rebuilt and the cult reinstated. This is often referred to as the Second Temple period. It continues right through until the destruction of the Temple by the Romans in AD 70. The Restoration should not be imagined simply as a return to how things were. While there was a return to Temple-centred worship, synagogues continued to have their own role, especially for those geographically removed from the Temple; and the Torah maintained its place as a controlling factor in Jewish life and religion, with the increasing dominance of those with authority to teach it (the scribes), and with an all too frequent drift towards legalism in interpretation and application.

The 1500 years from the days of Abraham to the time of Ezra (c. 1900–450 BC) saw many great changes in the form of worship in ancient Israel . . . If the form of worship changed with times and situations, its heart and centre did not. (G.J. Wenham, 'Worship', in *Marshall Pickering Encylcopedia of the Bible 2*, p. 2164)

Changing forms but consistent heart and centre. Israel's legitimate worship was always, whatever its actual form, a response to God's initiative and an expression of obedience to Him.

the one thing...

Andrew Maries

Balance up the corporate aspect of worship and understand that the presence of Jesus is not just found 'beyond
the veil' in an individual experience of personal and intimate worship. We're called to worship *together* as the
body of Christ. St Paul in Ephesians 1:23 says that the
church is 'the fulness of him who fills everything in every
way'. We're seriously losing this today and have been too
influenced by the individualistic, consumerist approach of
the rest of society. Let's begin to sing a lot more about
'we' rather than just 'I'.

What a Worship Leader Looks for in a Band

Tim Hughes

As a worship leader, it's essential to be a part of a team that gels together, are for each other, and get passionate about God together. Surround yourself with musicians and singers who are true worshippers. Being involved in a worship team is very different from being involved in a rock band. As a worship band your focus is on God, and leading His people into His presence. It is not about entertaining people with a few classic Christian hits. A worship band, by its very definition, must be made up of worshippers. This seems obvious, but in practice it can be so tempting to put the emphasis on the quality of musicianship, compromising heart standards for the sake of that long-sought-after drummer.

Next, find people who will buy into your vision and support what you're doing, both in their hearts and with their music. With these essential ingredients in place, here are some of the qualities I look for in a worship band.

I always start by looking at character. The attitude of

143

those involved is *always* more important than the gifting. First, do they walk humbly? It's so important that the worship team aren't up the front trying to impress people or feed their insecure egos. Again, it sounds fairly obvious, but you'd be surprised how many musicians have learned their craft in an environment where the emphasis is on impressing people. In worship though there is no room for performance. If I'm thinking about using someone on the worship team, first of all I observe them at church. Now I'm not talking about obsessively stalking them and tapping their phone, but about spending time with them, and looking to see if they really enter into worship on a regular basis. Also, how do they treat others in your church? These things are clues to a person's character. Of course, we must be careful, for ultimately who are we to judge? Yet a certain level of discernment is needed when looking to involve new people.

Then I look for a teachable heart. As part of a team you are always learning together. There are some very joyful times, but there are also some difficult things to face. Sometimes as a worship leader you may have to challenge some of your band members on an attitude issue. There is a great team-building dynamic when you are able to challenge someone and they take it on board humbly, instead of grudgingly or defensively. A friend of mine who leads worship once mentioned to a fairly experienced guitarist that he felt he needed to try and be more creative in his playing. This guitarist quickly took the advice on board and invested in lessons to improve his creativity. What a great example of a teachable spirit.

Next, I examine their attitude to others. Being involved in worship will inevitably mean being involved with a church, and to some degree we're all called to be pastors to the people we're leading. Every musician must work on their pastoral awareness. I love it when I see the musicians involve themselves with the people at the meetings. To me this models something very important. It demonstrates that everyone is working together and that just because someone is on a stage, it doesn't make them any more important.

Once you've looked at character, move on to musical gifting. Though not ultimately *the* most important factor in what worship leaders want from their band, this is a pretty important one. Someone may have the heart and the values, but if they can't play an instrument or sing in tune maybe their calling isn't to be on the worship team. At times I've played with people whose standard of play has actually distracted people's attention away from God and instead onto their hideously out of tune guitar or total lack of rhythm on the drums!

Look for creativity. I always love to be stretched creatively. Leading worship regularly, it's easy to become stale at times, so to have team members who keep challenging you to stay fresh musically is brilliant. Some musicians are very good at coming up with different sounds and ideas, and having them in the band can really stretch you as the worship leader.

I once heard someone say that if you have five members in a band, each one should play one-fifth of the overall music. The implication of this is that every band member needs to be a team player. It can be frustrating when musicians disappear into their own little world, totally unaware of what anyone else is playing. One sign of a team player is someone who is sensitive to noise levels on stage. Each member must keep their instrument to a level that serves the congregation and prefers the other members of the worship team.

At the end of the day, what you are looking for in a band is servants – people who will serve the church and support your leadership as together you worship God.

the one thing...

Daphne Rademaker

Let God be your defence and your advertiser. I continue to learn over and over that we don't need to make room for ourselves or strive to become a part of things. We just need to work on our craft and knock on God's door with what we have to offer.

We can give even when we are taken advantage of. And then go right back in and give again. There's a distinct difference between trying to gain favour with people and doing what God has asked us to do. Let's always do it God's way.

Worship with All You Have! (Psalm 100)

Don Williams

A psalm. For giving thanks.

1. Shout for joy to the Lord, all the earth.
2. Worship the Lord with gladness; come before him with joyful songs.
3. Know that the Lord is God. It is he who made us, and we are his; we are his people, the sheep of his pasture.
4. Enter his gates with thanksgiving and his courts with praise; give thanks to him and praise his name.
5. For the Lord is good and his love endures for ever; his faithfulness continues through all generations.

Worship with all you have! Worship is an event. We don't simply come to worship or attend worship; we do worship. This summons to worship in Psalm 100 is a summons to action: 'shout' (a shout of triumph or a battle cry), 'worship' (literally, 'serve', like a slave), 'come', 'enter', 'give thanks', 'praise'. When we do this, we throw our selves into it. It's hard to shout without using our whole body. We open our mouths, we fill our lungs, we let go. Again, when we enter Yahweh's gates with thanksgiving and His courts with praise, we are in motion. We are going somewhere – into the Temple to see the King. This worship, or service, is corporate, intense, loud, boisterous, energetic, releasing. It is worthy of our great God.

This kind of worship also has a tone. We shout 'for joy'. We worship 'with gladness'. We come with 'joyful songs'. We enter 'with thanksgiving and praise'. We 'give thanks to him', and 'praise his name'. Do you feel this? Exhilaration, gladness, exuberance, even ecstasy? Can you see faces: eyes wide open, expansive looks, brows raised, smiling, laughing – sweat-stained on a hot Jerusalem day? It is holy hilarity, worthy of majesty.

Psalm 100 is antiphonal. The worship leaders and the worshippers dialogue. This worship is active, reactive and dynamic. Unlike many of our churches, there are no passive observers here. The priests at the Temple gates summon the pilgrims: 'Shout for joy to the Lord, all the earth. Worship the Lord with gladness; come before him with joyful songs (vv. 1–2). The crowds respond with their confession: 'Know that the Lord is God. It is he who made us, and we are his; we are his people, the sheep of his pasture' (v. 3). Again, the priests call: 'Enter his gates with thanksgiving and his courts with praise; give thanks to him and praise his name' (v. 4). The people respond: 'For the Lord is good and his love endures for ever; his faithfulness continues through all generations' (v. 5).

Notice that the action of worship, the 'how?', is based

upon revelation, the 'why?'. We, and the whole earth, worship with such delight (vv. 1–2) because Yahweh ('the Lord') is God (implying all other gods are no gods, v. 3). He is our Creator; 'it is he who made us'. We are neither self-sufficient nor autonomous. He is our owner; 'we are his'. But He is also our Redeemer, calling us to be His covenant nation: 'we are his people, the sheep of his pasture' (kings in the ancient world were often symbolised as shepherds, see Psalm 23).

Again, the 'how?', we enter the Temple, give thanks to Him and praise His name (v. 4), because of the 'why?'. 'For the Lord [Yahweh] is good [steadfast in His moral character and justice] and his [covenant] love endures for ever; his faithfulness [trustworthiness] continues through all generations' (v. 5).

Does our worship measure up to these biblical tests? When we lead worship, do we expect things to happen? Are we participating in an event? Are we interacting with the worshippers we lead; is our worship dialogical? Does joy expressed by rejoicing in song mark our entrance into God's presence? Are we taking our people there? Is this joy mere emotion, or is it grounded in our creator, covenant King – with His attributes of goodness, eternal love and faithfulness through all generations?

Don't hold back. Worship costs us everything and we are made for exactly that. Our ancestors knew this: 'The chief end of man[kind] is to glorify God and enjoy him forever' (Westminster Shorter Catechism). Do we?

the one thing...

Paul Oakley

Sometimes the simple ideas are the best. The biggest challenge is to find a fresh way to express ancient truths that have already been written about for hundreds of years, and to find fresh ways to respond to and apply those things.

Content and Engagement

Matt Redman

When it comes to writing congregational song lyrics, it seems to me that two extremes often occur. Some worship songs take the 'heavy on content' route, packed full of biblical phrases and meaty theology; the kind of song that needs chewing on. Other songs take the opposite approach: simple, uncomplicated love songs, with a big emphasis placed on engaging with God.

There's definitely room for both types of song in our worship, and yet, as with so many things, it can be a little unhealthy if either of the two approaches is taken to the extreme. At one end of the spectrum you can write a song that is so wordy, crammed full of intricate theology and deep truth, that singing it unfortunately becomes simply an intellectual exercise rather than an outpouring of the heart. At the other extreme, it's also possible to write a worship song so raw and 'touchy-feely' in its approach that it captures no real sense of who God is, and therefore seems shallow.

The key is somehow to find a good balance between the 'content' and 'engagement' factors. I once heard someone comment on the well-known 'worship in spirit and truth' passage from John 4. They reflected that our worship songs need to have a sense of being a spiritual event, and yet also need to be clothed richly in the truth of who God is and what He has done. Some of the most valuable worship songs illuminate lyrically the beautiful truths of God, yet also give us space to reflect on, respond to and engage with Him.

I came across a scripture recently that I thought really suited this ideal. Over the last few months I've had my heart set on writing some simpler songs, and for me this portion of the Bible said it all. Ecclesiastes chapter 5 tells us: 'God is in heaven, and you are on earth, so let your words be few' (v. 2). Later on it urges us: 'Therefore stand in awe of God' (v. 7).

In this chapter of the Bible, in just over twenty words, is a fantastic song-birthing piece of truth. Of course there's a time to excitedly express to God everything that's on our hearts, the overflow of hearts of love and wonder. Yet there's also a time to quieten down and simply stand in awe of Him with the simplest of songs and the fewest of words.

So how do we pursue a healthy balance of content and engagement in our quest to write God-honouring, church-friendly worship songs? First of all, make sure the song starts off as worship. It seems obvious to say this, but if a song is written to end up in worship, then it must be birthed in worship. Maybe the Holy Spirit has been highlighting a particular theme in your church, which has begun to burn in your own heart. Find space to respond to God around that theme, and worship Him. A song that starts off as little more than a cerebral exercise will probably end up being no more than that in a congregation. But a song that begins its life as a passionate time of engaging with God will hopefully carry that same dynamic with it into a congregational setting.

And then comes the perspiration. Once the initial inspiration has been poured out, most songs need to be crafted and worked on before they are suitable for congregational use. Spend time being ruthless with your lyrics. There are always lots more options available to you than you may first realise. Take the theme of the song and begin studying it. There are many ways to do this. One easy way is to find a concordance and simply look up the song's theme to see if any other scriptures are suitable for your lyrics. It's a great way to have a Bible study. You might also refer to some old hymns and see if they inspire you with fresh ideas as you pursue the theme of your song.

One thing to keep in mind is that 'simple' doesn't have to mean 'shallow'. I've been challenging myself to write songs that are short enough to be memorised quickly, yet have some sort of depth to the lyrics in terms of the revelation of Jesus. Let's aim to write songs that reveal something of the wonderful mysteries of God, and at the same time give the worshipper space to respond to Him simply and wholeheartedly.

the one thing...

Andy Piercy

Spend time learning the craft of songwriting. Not many people write their best songs straight away. Your song-writing will benefit enormously from time and effort being given to it. Just because the best songwriters make it appear easy, don't be fooled into thinking that it is. Remember the '10 per cent inspiration and 90 per cent perspiration' rule. Even inspired songs usually benefit from a refining process.

And don't feel you have to make every song idea work. Always remember that the widely sung songs are just the cream of the crop. Even your favourite writers come up with stuff that simply gets thrown away.

Understanding Worship: Part 4

Chris Jack

The heart of worship in the Old Testament

Contrary to a popular misconception, worship is more than its external form in the Old Testament. Although at times great attention is given to the rituals involved, mere ritual is never acceptable on its own, however outwardly correct it might be. There is in fact throughout the Old Testament a constant emphasis on the worshipper having the right attitude of heart towards God if his or her worship is to be acceptable. Having a right heart before God, or 'personal piety', is a prerequisite for all true worship.

> Personal piety then is the one necessary precondition for all Hebrew worship, the formal and the informal, the spontaneous and the structured, the individual and the corporate. (Andrew Hill)

The Old Testament has a great deal to say about false worship. False worship involves one of three things:

1. IDOLATRY – worshipping the wrong thing
2. FORMALISM – worshipping with the wrong heart/attitude
3. HYPOCRISY – worship divorced from appropriate lifestyle

Idolatry was rampant in the nations surrounding Israel. In essence, idolatry is the worship of anyone or anything but the one true God. In practice, idolatry frequently took the form of the worship of false gods, usually in the form of images of some kind. It was also often bound up with immoral practices such as ritual prostitution, child sacrifice, etc. Tragically, idolatrous worship frequently found its way into Israelite worship. Sometimes this was in a full-blown way, but more commonly it involved some form of syncretism – in other words, preserving elements of legitimate worship but blending in extraneous and illegitimate elements from Canaanite and other systems.

Worship of anything other than the one true God is prohibited by the first commandment (Exodus 20:3), while the worship of any image of any kind is forbidden by the second (Exodus 20:4–6). Further denunciations of idols and idolatry abound in the Old Testament (e.g. Leviticus 26:1; Deuteronomy 27:15; 1 Samuel 15:23; 1 Kings 14:9; Psalm 78:58; Isaiah 42:17; Jeremiah 7:30; Ezekiel 14:4; 23:49). Idolatry is also expressly repudiated in the New Testament (1 Corinthians 10:14; Galatians 5:20; Colossians 3:5; 1 Peter 4:3).

So worshipping other gods, deflecting worship from the one true God, is clearly unacceptable. An equally unacceptable approach to worship, however, is that which preserves the externals but reduces reality to ritual. Mere formalism – going through the motions, performing the correct rituals, but without the corresponding right attitude of heart – is condemned as vigorously as idolatry (Psalms 24:3–6; 51:16–17 [cf. vv. 6, 10f.]; Isaiah 66:1–4). Conversely, praise is to be offered not merely with the lips but with one's whole being (Psalms 45:1; 103:1 [cf. Isaiah 29:13]; Jeremiah 12:2).

A further type of false worship is that which is not accompanied by a corresponding life of obedience to God's commands. Failing to live in a way that is consistent with being in relationship with God while outwardly offering worship to Him is pure hypocrisy. This is also roundly condemned (1 Samuel 15:22f.; Jeremiah 7:21–24; Amos 5:21–24 [cf. vv. 7–12]. See also Psalms 40:6–10; 50:13–15). These passages are very sobering and are worth taking time to read and reflect on. At first sight it seems strange that at times God should appear to despise or reject the very sacrificial system He had given. However, the truth is that it is not the cult itself that God is speaking against but its abuse. Quite simply, doing the right thing with the wrong motives is just not good enough.

The heart of worship is heart worship. And we are still in the Old Testament! What a message and challenge there is for us at a time when *how* we worship has become such a dominant and problematic issue. The Old Testament reminds us in very clear terms that acceptable worship is always more about the attitude than the approach. The Israelites seemed to get it wrong so often. We need perhaps to ask ourselves whether we really do any better.

So what is the heart of worship in the Old Testament? A number of key principles stand out.

1. Worship is relational. It involves engagement with a personal God.
2. Worship is required of all humanity by creation and of God's people by calling.
3. Worship is a response to God's initiatives in both revelation and redemption.
4. Worship involves submission, service and reverence.
5. Worship has both individual and corporate expressions.
6. Worship may be informal as well as formal.
7. Worship changes in form yet is constant in its essence.
8. Worship is about attitude not just activity.
9. Worship is holistic: it involves the whole person.
10. Worship is life(style) as well as liturgy.

There is one point that is perhaps worth underlining here: a strong emphasis on obedience runs through the Old Testament. As noted above, worship is a response to God's initiatives. And this response, if it is to be acceptable, must always be on His terms. It is true that in the time of the Patriarchs the formal requirements for worship were much less detailed and stringent than in later periods. Yet even for Abraham and the others, God's instructions were to be obeyed when given (cf. Genesis 15, 17). The theme of obedience is central to the message of the book of Deuteronomy, both in relation to the keeping of the Law in general and in the context of offering to God acceptable worship.

Many passages could be cited here. However, one tragic story from the life of Saul highlights perhaps better than any other the seriousness of this issue. It is to be found in 1 Samuel 15. The chapter is worth reading. It is tragic-comical in the way it is recounted and is in its own right a superb example of Hebrew story-telling at its best. The core of the story is that Saul seeks to justify not carrying out God's instructions to destroy the Amalekites totally (including livestock) by protesting that he has saved the best in order to offer it in sacrifice to God (1 Samuel 15:20f.). The response of Samuel, the prophet sent by God to confront Saul, is stinging:

> 'Does the LORD delight in burnt offerings and sacrifices as much as in obeying the voice of the LORD? To obey is better than sacrifice, and to heed is better than the fat of rams. For rebellion is like the sin of divination, and arrogance like the evil of idolatry. Because you have rejected the word of the LORD, he has rejected you as king.' (1 Samuel 15:22f.)

Worship is to be offered to God on His terms, in accordance with His instructions, in the context of a life submitted to Him and obedient to His revealed will and ways. Nothing else is acceptable.

> Obedience to God in cultic observance was to go hand in hand with obedience in matters of everyday life. (David Peterson, *Engaging with God*, IVP, 2002, p. 49)

The people of the Old Testament could not simply do it their way. And, of course, neither can we.

the one thing...

Rick Cua

The thing that has motivated me most over the years is a call to excellence. Not someone else's version of excellence, but your own. No matter what your skill level is in traditional standards, there is something about operating at the top of your gifting. Nothing can be more distracting than the realisation that someone is just getting by because of a lack of passion.

You can have the best equipment, the best songs to play and a special moment to lead worship, but without the development of your skill from the inside out, you risk missing the fullness that God has ordained for that moment.

Cultivating a Quiet Heart

Matt Redman

The 1960s (so I hear) were a pretty crazy time for music. At the height of all this madness, the Beatles were huge, playing to crowds of tens of thousands. Unfortunately, some of the sound equipment couldn't quite compete with the thousands of screaming fans back then, and they soon decided to give up playing live. As Paul McCartney explained, 'We were getting worse and worse as a band while all those people were screaming . . . It was lovely that they liked us, but we couldn't hear to play.'

Now most of us don't have to put up with crowds of people screaming, but there are plenty of other distractions that come into play for someone involved in leading worship. So my question to myself recently has been, 'Can I still hear to play?' Or in other words, 'Am I finding enough space and peace in my life to hear the voice of the Lord prompting me and the song of the Lord inspiring me?' As lead worshippers, it's essential we find space to breathe, time to think and moments to listen to the still small voice.

In Psalm 131:2 the writer declares, 'I have stilled . . . my soul.' Eugene Peterson's *The Message* rephrases it: 'I have cultivated a quiet heart.' And that ultimately is what we're talking about here. There are so many different noises in our lives that can drown out the whispers of God. As I heard Bill Hybels (Willow Creek, Chicago) once ask: 'Is the ambient noise level of my life low enough for me to hear the whispers of the Lord?' That's a great question.

Richard Swenson, in his book *Margin*, talks about the pain of overload and lists a few specific areas where our lives are getting a little too noisy. Here are a couple:

Activity overload – Often we end up being so busy that we try and do two or three things at once. (Ever seen someone driving their car whilst on the phone, eating a sandwich, and reading a magazine?)

Choice overload – In 1978 there were 11,767 items in the average USA supermarket. By 1992 that number had risen to 24,531 (including 186 different types of breakfast cereal found in one store).

Joseph Piper, in his book *Only the Lover Sings*, puts it like this:

Man's ability to see is in decline. Searching for the reasons we could point to several things: modern man's restlessness and stress . . . or his total enslavement by practical goals and purposes. Yet one reason must not be overlooked either: the average person of our time loses the ability to see because there is too much to see.

I know this is true for me. Too often I've found myself rushing around like crazy, and then filling up my precious few rest times with flicking through meaningless TV programmes. Of course, we all have responsibilities in life, and it's great to have some leisure time to bring a balance. But if I'm consistently finding there's no space to listen out for the 'song of the Lord', then something might have to change. Creativity and the prophetic are so often birthed in the place of stillness. So often when I'm struggling to bring something fresh in the congregation, it's because I've had no time refreshing my soul before God.

Andrew Murray (in the book *Waiting on God*) looks at a couple of verses on this whole theme of stillness. Lamentations 3:26 tells us, 'It is good to wait quietly for the salvation of the Lord.' Then, in Isaiah 30:15, we hear, 'In quietness and trust is your strength.' Murray says of these two scriptures, 'Such words reveal to us the close connection between quietness and faith. And show us what a deep need there is of quietness as an element of waiting on God.'

Let us be a people who seek to cultivate a quiet heart, listening constantly for the inspiring whispers of the Lord. So often He is in the still small voice.

the one thing...

Noel Richards

Ask God to birth a big vision in your heart for the things He wants you to do. Allow Him to fire your imagination and put dreams within you for the sake of the kingdom. God is looking for a generation of musicians, singers, dancers, writers, poets and prophets who will touch the nations with the sounds of heaven.

Renewing the Intimate Friendship

Matt Redman

With worship leading it's not *what* you know but *who* you know. I've been reminded of that recently. After a busy few months I found myself a victim once again of the Martha syndrome: so busy with the preparations and serving that I'd somehow neglected the better thing – sitting at the feet of Jesus, listening devotedly as Mary did (Luke 10:38–42).

Don't get me wrong, I still knew how to raise my hands in the air, and I could still remember the words, chords and melodies of the songs. But it's so easy for these meaningful expressions of worship to become empty, outward habits. It's not *what* you know – any knowledge or experience of worship or worship leading that may have been gained means nothing at such a time – it's *who* you know. I want every word and every note to be an expression of relationship with God.

Worship in its truest form is all about relationship. In the Westminster Shorter Catechism the chief end of man is defined as: 'To glorify God and to enjoy Him for ever'.

First, to *glorify*. In other words, to respond to this wonderful God with our lives, our deeds, our thoughts, our words and our songs. And, at the same time, to *enjoy* Him. As John Piper reminds us, God is most glorified in us when we are most satisfied in Him.

The Lord has called us to an intimate relationship with Himself. It would be an honour to merely stand from afar and revere the King of kings with our songs of praise. Yet He has called us to something deeper: a friendship with Him. This is the King of Revelation chapter 1, who majestically holds the seven stars in His right hand. Yet He is the same King who in the very next verse draws near to the writer, John, and touches him with the same right hand, comforting him and saying, 'Do not be afraid.' And the more we revere Jesus as this awesome King, the more we realise the wonder of the hand of friendship He extends to us.

Now and again we find ourselves in a place where we've lost our focus. Maybe there's been too much output without enough input. Maybe we're so busy that we've become distracted. I've met so many musicians in that place, and I've been there myself. God calls us back to the place of friendship.

In John 15:15 Jesus tells His disciples, 'I no longer call you servants . . . I have called you friends.' Now of course we're all meant to serve Him, but God is calling us deeper, to the place of friendship; a place where a mere servant could never go. Make sure, as a lead worshipper, you've not just settled for the role of servant, when a friendship with Almighty God is on offer.

It's time to renew the intimate friendship. Do what you must, as soon as you can. For in the end, with worship leading it's never really about *what* you know; it's all about *who* you know.

Imagine the View from Here

John David Walt, Jr

Leading worship is about seeing God. The life of a worshipper, and particularly the life of a lead worshipper, is far more about a quality of vision than it is a type of personality or set of gifts. Before you can worship God you must first see God. Worship and leading worship are about seeing God. The greatest worshippers of all time, the history-makers, saw the Lord. They had a vision of God: 'The word of the Lord came to Abram in a vision' (Genesis 15:1). Glimpsing God's glory, even from behind, empowered Moses to go forward, leading the Israelites in worship. Listen to Isaiah: 'In the year that King Uzziah died, I saw the Lord seated on a throne, high and exalted, and the train of his robe filled the temple.' From Judges to Kings, through the Prophets and onward to the Apostles, what separates their life and work from the rest, which is to say what distinguishes their worship, is a quality of vision. They saw God and could never return to the ordinary again. And compelled by the vision of God, others followed.

Down through the centuries, the saints are set apart by their vision of God. Hear Bernard of Clairvaux on worship: 'Jesus the very thought of thee with sweetness fills the breast; but sweeter far thy face to see, and in thy presence rest.'[1] Thomas Aquinas, easily the greatest theologian of the medieval era, gave his life to the pursuit of the knowledge of God. The staggering influence of his scholarship is breath-taking. On 6 December 1273, while attending Mass, Thomas had a vision of God. Upon being asked to write about it he responded, 'Such things have been revealed to me that all that I have written seems to me as so much straw. Now I await the end of my life.'[2] He never wrote again. In 1393, Julian of Norwich completed *Revelations of Divine Love*, a written account of her sixteen visions of Jesus. The list goes on.

Leading worship is about seeing God. From hymns like 'Be Thou my vision', to choruses such as 'Open our eyes, Lord, we want to see Jesus', to our modern worship songs like 'Open the eyes of my heart, Lord' and 'I want to see you . . . high and lifted up, shining in the light of Your glory'[3] our quest in worship is to see God. But what is this about? In the days of the Old Testament, the question was always how one could see God and live. Today the question may be how one can see God and stay out of the psychiatric ward. So what does it mean to see God and, more importantly, how does it happen in a way leading to an abandoned life of worship?

There is no formula. This is not a practical essay. Worship is not practical. Contemporary theologian,

Marva Dawn, calls worship 'a royal waste of time'. Worshipping God and leading others to worship Him comes from the capacity of a holy imagination. The idea is not new or original, but it could be revolutionary. Worship is born from an imagination, rooted in remembrance, cultivated through attention and nurtured by discipline.

The great preachers, poets and prophets, the great songwriters and singers, were those who lived imaginatively from a vision of God. Because they saw, their leadership transformed people's ears into eyes. Hearing gives way to seeing, and worship literally combusts into vision. Imagine. Isn't this what a lead worshipper does? It's not about singing songs, but about seeing God and calling others into the vision. The lead worshipper stands, no kneels, at all the places of the wonder of God and says simply and creatively, 'Imagine the view from here.' The lead worshipper journeys through the stunning story of God, stopping at all the scenic overlooks, and gazes on the revealed horizon of God's glory and says clearly and profoundly, 'Imagine the view from here.'

Beginning at the utter ends of the cosmos, imagine the view from here:

Immortal, Invisible, God only wise;
in light inaccessible hid from our eyes.[4]
Into the wonder of creation . . . *You spread out Your*
arms over empty space,
said 'Let there be light' in a dark and formless place the
world was born . . .

What a wonderful Maker.
Shout to the Lord, all the Earth let us sing,
power and majesty praise to the King.
Mountains bow down and the seas will roar
at the sound of Your Name.[5]
Imagine the view from here.

Through the pain of rebellion and exile, imagine the view from here:

We bow our hearts, we bend our knees,
O Spirit come make us humble.
We turn our eyes from evil things. O Lord we cast down
our idols.
Give us clean hands and give us pure hearts,
let us not lift our soul to another.[6]
Imagine the view from here.

To the place of mercy, imagine the view from here:

When I survey the wondrous cross,
on which the Prince of Glory died . . .
I'm forgiven because You were forsaken.
I'm accepted. You were condemned.
Open up the skies of mercy,
rain down the cleansing flood . . .
It's Your kindness, Lord, that leads us to repentance . . .
It's Your beauty, Lord,
that makes us stand in silence.
Your love is better than life.[7]

Imagine the view from here.

And onward in the pilgrimage to the house of God, imagine the view from here:

Now You are exalted to the highest place,
King of the heavens, where one day I'll bow.
How lovely is Your dwelling place, O Lord Almighty.
My soul longs and even faints for You.
For here my heart is satisfied within Your presence.
I sing beneath the shadow of Your wings.
Better is one day in Your courts than a thousand
elsewhere.[8]
Imagine the view from here.

And outward as apostles to the whole world, imagine the view from here:

Open up the doors, let the music play,
let the streets resound with singing.
Songs that bring Your hope; songs that bring Your joy;
dancers who dance upon injustice . . .[9]
Imagine the view from here.

Taking with us as many as will come upward to the place where the streets have no name, imagine the view from here:

We fall down. We lay our crowns at the feet of Jesus . . .
and we cry Holy, Holy, Holy is the Lamb.

Surrounded by Your glory, what will my heart feel?
Will I dance for You, Jesus, or in awe of You be still?
Will I stand in Your presence or to my knees will I fall?
Will I sing Hallelujah? Will I be able to speak at all?
I can only imagine.[10]
Imagine the view from here.

Biographies

Brenton Brown is the writer of 'Lord, reign in me' and 'Your love is amazing', among other Vineyard songs. Living in Oxford, where he heads up the worship team, he also travels widely, teaching on and leading worship.

Dave Clifton is based at Holy Trinity Brompton in London, and writes many worship songs, including the co-written 'Praise God from whom all blessings flow' with Andy Piercy. Dave has also had a great deal of experience as a musical director with various artists and bands.

Rick Cua, though still active as a bass player and songwriter, currently serves as Vice-President, Creative, at EMI Christian Music Publishing. Married to his high school sweetheart, Diana, for thirty-one years, Rick and Diana live in Brentwood, Tennessee, and have two daughters, Niki and Nina.

Brian Doerksen lives in Abbotsford BC, Canada, with his wife Joyce and their six children. The writer of songs such as 'Come, now is the time', 'Faithful One' and 'Refiner's fire', he regularly encourages others in the craft of composing congregational worship songs.

Wayne Drain is married to June, with three children. He is the senior pastor at Fellowship of Christians in Arkansas, a church he founded with some friends in the early 1970s during the Jesus Movement, and leads worship and speaks regularly in various countries.

Louie Giglio and his wife Shelley head up the Passion movement in the USA, and its music label, Six Steps records. With a desire for 'the name and the renown' of the Lord (Isaiah 26:8) they encourage thousands of college students in their pursuit of true worship.

Charlie Groves is married to Ali and they have three children. Since April 1999 he has been working as a worship pastor at Church of the Holy Spirit, a recent church plant in Cape Town, South Africa. Before this he was a worship leader at Holy Trinity Brompton Anglican church in London, England.

Charlie Hall is married to Kimberlyn, and with their two children they live in Oklahoma City. Ministering all over the USA with Passion, Charlie's songs include the well-known worship anthem 'Salvation'.

Tim Hughes is the writer of 'Here I am to worship', as well as many other congregational songs. Based at Watford in England, he travels with Soul Survivor encouraging young people around the world to 'know Jesus and make Him known'.

Chris Jack lives in Cambridge, England, and is Chaplain and Lecturer in Applied Theology at London Bible College. Specialising in a theology of worship, he regularly instructs students there in the biblical foundations of our corporate worship.

Song and hymn writer **Graham Kendrick** has written over 500 worship compositions, including the very widely sung 'Shine, Jesus, shine' and 'The Servant King'. A regular writer and speaker on the subject of worship song content, he is married to Gill and lives in Surrey, England.

Based in Nashville, Tennessee, **Tom Lane** and his wife Patty are part of Belmont Church. Ministering with the Bridge, Tom longs to see creative young musicians affirmed in their callings, while his own songs have been resourced through Worship Together, Integrity and Maranatha.

Martyn Layzell regularly leads worship at Soul Survivor events, and is an assistant pastor at the Soul Survivor church in Watford. Married to Emily, he is the writer of songs such as 'Not by words' and 'Sovereign Lord'.

Based in Devon, England, **Andrew Maries** works through the Keynote Trust to encourage and stimulate music and worship across the churches at every level and in every style.

Robin Mark lives in Belfast with his wife Jacqueline and three children. He has led worship in his local church, Christian Fellowship Church in Belfast, for some nine years now. Robin is also a successful businessman, heading up his own company F.R. Mark and Associates.

Les Moir is head of Survivor Records in the UK, and works closely with various youth organisations to resource the church with fresh worship songs and sounds. He is also a bass player and former producer of worship albums by Graham Kendrick, Noel Richards and Matt Redman.

Sally Morgenthaler is President of SJM Management Company, Inc., and functions as on-site worship consultant for Denver Seminar and Pathways Church. She has written books and articles, and regularly teaches on worship in a postmodern culture.

Nigel Morris was born in the UK and moved to the US in 1991 with his wife Lynne and their daughter Sarah. He is on the staff at Anaheim Vineyard, where he oversees both the Worship Music department and the prison ministry.

Steve Nicholson is on the leadership board of the Vineyard movement in the USA, and pastors a church in Evanston, Illinois. A strong encourager of many lead worshippers, his leadership expertise brings wisdom and insight to the lives of many.

Based at Church of Christ the King, Brighton, **Paul Oakley** regularly leads worship at the 1,000-strong church and with his band heads up the worship at many NFI youth events. His songs include 'It's all about You' ('Jesus, lover of my soul') and 'Because of You'.

Graham Ord has been leading worship for nearly twenty years. He has recorded several CDs with the Vineyard Music Group, as well as for several solo projects. He is now based in Vancouver, BC, where he works as a singer/songwriter and worship leader. He also speaks at conferences and training events on worship and songwriting.

Andy Park is worship overseer of the North Langley Vineyard in Canada. Writer of 'Only You' and numerous other Vineyard worship songs, he is also the author of *To Know You More – Cultivating the Heart of the Worship Leader*.

Andrew Philip, originally from South Africa, now lives in the UK. A producer, keyboard player and programmer player for the likes of Soul Survivor and Vineyard, he is also part of the heartofworship.com website team.

Andy Piercy is the music director at Holy Trinity Brompton in London. Producer of albums by Rita Springer, Promise Keepers, Matt Redman and Cutting Edge (aka Delirious), he has a great deal of experience in overseeing the crafting and developing of congregational songs.

Mike Pilavachi leads Soul Survivor, a worship-centred youth movement working with young people around the world. Having mentored many lead worshippers, written the book *The Audience of One* and spoken regularly at various worship gatherings, worship is without a doubt Mike's 'specialist subject'.

Daphne Rademaker lives in Langley, Canada, with her husband Darryl, where she leads worship at the Vineyard church. Daphne has also sung on many of the Vineyard Music releases.

Matt Redman is married to Beth and together they are part of Church of Christ the King in Brighton, England. Matt is the writer of 'Heart of worship', 'Let my words be few' and 'Befriended', as well as author of *The Unquenchable Worshipper*. He is part of the team that edits the heartofworship.com website.

Noel Richards and his wife Tricia are based at Pioneer People in Surrey. Writer of songs such as 'All heaven declares' and 'To be in Your presence', in 1997 he co-ordinated the Champion of the World worship event at Wembley Stadium.

David Salmon is a musician, playwright, artist and graphic designer based at Soul Survivor, Watford, in England. Through Littleboat Productions David and his wife Rosemary pursue many ways to build bridges between worship and the arts. David designed *The Heart of Worship Files* book cover.

Kathryn Scott is married to Alan, and they live in Ireland, pastoring the Causeway Coast Vineyard. Kathryn leads worship on VMG's *Hungry* and *Surrender* CDs.

Rita Springer lives in Houston and devotes much of her time and focus specifically to ministering to women. Involved with the Vineyard Music Group, she has written numerous songs, as well as being involved globally in various conferences.

Texan **Chris Tomlin** regularly leads worship as part of the Passion team, alongside Louie Giglio. Writer of songs such as 'We fall down' and 'The wonderful cross', Chris and his band travel around the world leading the people of God in worship, and teaching others as they do the same.

Tommy Walker has led worship throughout the United States, Canada, Europe and Asia. Graduating in 1982 from Christ For The Nations Institute with a degree in practical theology, he gained a diploma in jazz and fusion at the Guitar Institute of Technology in Hollywood, California.

John David Walt, Jr is Vice-President of Community Life and Dean of the Chapel at Asbury Theological Seminary in Kentucky. Co-writer of 'The wonderful cross' with Chris Tomlin (and Isaac Watts!), he is also involved with the Passion movement of college students throughout the USA.

UK bass player **Matt Weeks** has been on worship teams with the likes of Brian Doerksen, Matt Redman, Brenton Brown and Tim Hughes. Also able to play drums, trumpet, guitar and keyboards, Matt is in an ideal position to give insight into the many aspects of playing on a worship team.

Californian theologian **Don Williams** and his wife Kathryn live in San Diego, where he has just retired as a Vineyard pastor. A former Hollywood pastor, and Professor of New Testament at Fuller Theological Seminary, Don's activities now include working alongside Matt Redman in training young worship leaders in songwriting and theology.

John Willison is the worship pastor at the Evanston Vineyard in Chicago, Illinois. Married to Carol, he is the writer of several Vineyard worship songs, including 'My Redeemer lives' and 'Jesus, I believe in You'.

Based at Hillsong in Australia, **Darlene Zschech** is writer of 'Shout to the Lord', one of the most universally sung worship songs in recent years. Married to Mark, she has recently written the book *Extravagant Worship*, and also serves as Executive Director of Mercy Ministries Australia, a Christ-centred residential programme for girls and women who suffer from eating disorders, drug addiction and emotional/physical abuse.

Notes

Worship and Addiction

1. Worship = to fall down. Psalm 95:6 'Let us worship and bow down.' Documentation in Donald M. Williams, *The Communicator's Commentary Series*, Old Testament, Volume 14: Psalms 73–150, Lloyd J. Ogilvie, ed. (Dallas, TX: Word, 1989), p. 193.
2. Gerald G. May, *Addiction and Grace* (San Francisco, CA: Harper San Francisco, 1988), p. 4.
3. John Bradshaw, *Bradshaw on the Family* (Deerfield Beach, FL: Health Communications, Inc., 1988), p. 20.
4. Tom Wright, *New Tasks for a Renewed Church*, published in the US as *Bringing the Church to the World* (Minneapolis, MN: Bethany House, 1992), pp. 44–51.

The Cross: Exploring All Angles

1. Martin Kahler, *The So-Called Historical Jesus and the*

Historic Biblical Christ (Philadelphia, PA: Fortress Press, 1964), p. 80 n. 11, cited by John T. Carrol and Joel B. Green, *The Death of Jesus in Early Christianity* (Peabody, Mass: Hendrickson, 1995), p. 55.

2. Leon Morris, *The Apostolic Preaching of the Cross* (Grand Rapids, MI: Eerdmans, 1956), pp. 49, 98, 114, 196, 248, 258.

3. N. T. Wright, *Jesus and the Victory of God* (Minneapolis, MN: Fortress, 1996), pp. 154–155.

4. P. T. Forsyth, cited by Leon Morris, *The Apostolic Preaching of the Cross*, p. 220. Forsyth's original is in *The Work of Christ* (London, 1948), p. 105.

5. James Denney, *The Death of Christ* (New Canaan, CT: Keats Publishing, Inc., 1981), pp. 177–178.

Imagine the View from Here

1. Bernard of Clairvaux, "Jesu dulcis memoria," trans. Edward Caswall, "Jesus, the Very Thought of Thee."

2. Source unknown.

3. These lyrics come from the following songs: Mary E. Byrne, trans., "Be Thou My Vision"; Robert Cull, "Open Our Eyes, Lord"; Paul Baloche, "Open the Eyes of My Heart."

4. Walter Chalmers Smith, "Immortal, Invisible, God Only Wise."

5. These lyrics come from the following songs: Matt Redman, "Wonderful Maker"; Darlene Zschech, "Shout to the Lord."

6. Charlie Hall, "Give Us Clean Hands."

7. These lyrics come from the following songs: Isaac Watts, "When I Survey the Wondrous Cross"; Billy Foote, "You Are My King"; Chris Tomlin, Jesse Reeves and Louie Giglio, "Kindness."

8. These lyrics come from the following songs: Matt Redman, "Once Again"; Matt Redman, "Better Is One Day."

9. Martin Smith, "Did You Feel the Mountains Tremble."

10. These lyrics come from the following songs: Chris Tomlin, "We Fall Down"; Bart Millard, "I Can Only Imagine."

The Unquenchable Worshipper

by Matt Redman

This book is about a kind of worshipper:

> *Unquenchable. Undivided.*
> *Unpredictable.*

On a quest to bring glory and pleasure to God, these worshippers will not allow themselves to be distracted or defeated:

> *Unstoppable. Undignified.*
> *Undone.*

Worshippers who long for their hearts, lives and songs to be the kind of offerings God is looking for.

'This is unashamedly a book about God and living a devoted life in His presence. Worship is *about* God, *to* God and *for* God. *The Unquenchable Worshipper* shouts this truth out loud.'

Mike Pilavachi, Soul Survivor

survivor

survivor ...worship for a new generation

The Father's Song
Matt Redman
CD - SURCD038
Cassette - SURC038

Intimacy
Matt Redman
CD - SURCD008
Cassette - SURC008

**The Friendship
& the Fear**
Matt Redman
CD - SURCD001
Cassette - SURC001

**Passion for Your
Name & Wake up
my soul**
Matt Redman
CD - SURCD040
Cassette - SURC040

Undignified
Soul Survivor
CD - SURCD041

The Message
Soul Survivor
CD - SURCD045
Cassette - SURC045